CONSTITUTIONAL
BRICOLAGE

GERALD GARVEY

CONSTITUTIONAL
BRICOLAGE

PRINCETON UNIVERSITY PRESS

PRINCETON, NEW JERSEY 1971

Publication of this book has been aided by
the Whitney Darrow Publication Reserve Fund
of Princeton University Press

This book has been composed in Caledonia
Printed in the United States of America by
Princeton University Press, Princeton, New Jersey

This book is dedicated to

my Mother and my Father

CONTENTS

In which is outlined an approach to constitutional interpretation focusing not on substantive Supreme Court doctrine, but on judicial form in a threefold sense: (1) certain standard forms in which Court opinions are cast; (2) sources of constitutional doctrine in standard formulas for resolving recurrent problems; and (3) use of these formulas to link judges' decisions with basic norms of the political culture.

In which is presented a framework for analysis of American constitutional development—a view of society and of the often informal rules that hold society together—based on certain modes of social interaction which are universal in human experience but variable in form and importance from culture to culture, and especially on an analysis of the buyer-seller or "exchange" and the ruler-subject or "power" modes.

In which it is shown that the main working parts of the U.S. political system can be analyzed as buyer-seller and ruler-subject transactions between people and government, suggesting that the rules governing these transactions, applied in light of the framers' concepts of the nature and purposes of power, provided the basis of U.S. constitutional limitations. A chapter appendix discusses separation of powers and federalism.

PREFACE

EXCEPT for the word *bricolage*, introduced by the anthropologist Levi-Strauss in *The Savage Mind* (1962), there is little new in this thesis. The exposition that follows relies on received anthropological and sociological theory, especially of the "functionalist" and "cultural" schools. Nor is identification of the buyer-seller mode as the traditional organizing principle of American constitutional interpretation a departure from the established view in political science. Some of the most influential contributions of twentieth-century constitutional historians and critics have emphasized the interpenetration of an economic—mercantile, property-biased—culture with America's legal fabric. What may be surprising, however, is the extent to which analysis of America's constitutional tradition from the perspective of "social sciences" that were not even separate disciplines when Beard and Corwin began publishing has led to conclusions consistent with those of traditionalist writers.

Much of the substantive material in this volume came to me from Corwin's student and my own teacher, Alpheus T. Mason of Princeton, who must already know the extent of my affection for and debt to him. Additionally, my colleague Walter F. Murphy read the entire manuscript and gave me many suggestions. I must also thank Sandy Thatcher of Princeton University Press for his help and forbearance; Mrs. Dorothy Sylvester, my typist, for much help "above and beyond the call"; Mrs. Reba Titus, my secretary; Messrs. John Buerkle and Peter Rossiter, my research assistants and students at Princeton, for invaluable citation-checking; and the several sections of undergraduates, mostly in Princeton's Classes of 1969 and 1970, on whom I have from time to time inflicted portions of the thesis contained herein. My greatest thanks of all are due, of course, to my wife LouAnn.

Detroit Lakes, Minnesota
July 1970

CONSTITUTIONAL
BRICOLAGE

It is possible that the requirement of "totalization" is a great novelty to some historians, sociologists and psychologists. It has been taken for granted by anthropologists ever since they learned it from Malinowski. But Malinowski's deficiencies have also taught us that this is not where explanation ends. It only begins when we have succeeded in constituting our object. The role of dialectical reason is to put the human sciences in possession of a reality with which it alone can furnish them, but the properly scientific work consists in decomposing and then recomposing on a different plane.

Claude Levi-Strauss, from
The Savage Mind, Chapter IX

INTRODUCTION

Society may be viewed as a web of transactions through which values are distributed among individuals and groups. Repetitive social transactions generate regularized modes of behavior. Certain modes become dominant and form the characteristic features of a given society. The transaction between buyer and seller—generically considered—is usually thought to be modal for the United States and is reflected in the primacy of mercantile activities, in such legal values as sanctity of contract, and even in the use of marketplace analogies in the constitutional law of free speech. (The best test of an idea, Holmes argued, is its ability to get accepted in the marketplace.)

All societies legislate rules—even if only informally—to govern the common transactions of day-to-day life. These customary rules underlie much of law. Thus law is brought into harmony with the broader culture. Achievement of cultural coherence in this way is like the process through which an individual, following rules of syntax, organizes the different parts of speech into a coherent sentence. We may speak therefore of "social syntax," referring to a strain toward coherence in norms, attitudes, and beliefs that is reflected in behavior.

Rules to govern transactions grow round the dominant principle of a given culture—for example, the buyer-seller or "exchange" or "contract" principle as the preferred mode of allocating rights, wealth, and power. Since these transactions determine the allocation of values, and since law reflects the rules and influences allocations normatively, identification of the society's "syntactical" principle furnishes a key to its constitutional processes. This reflection in law of a deeper cultural unity helps give continuity to constitutional interpretation.

But such continuity takes its price. It limits both judicial freedom and legislative discretion. Pressures toward syntax determine, for lawgivers as well as for laymen, certain forms of acceptable behavior. Thus as long ago as 1610 Coke argued in the *Bonham* case, which adumbrated judicial review, that a law contrary to reason is void. "Reason" meant the accepted usages of the realm.

In a society ideally patterned on the buyer-seller or exchange transaction, freedom and sanctity of contract would be opposite sides of one absolute value—as, indeed, they virtually were for Chief Justice Marshall and for many of his nineteenth-century laissez-faire successors. Representative of such a culture is J. D. MacHardie, the tycoon in John O'Hara's novel *From the Terrace* (1959). This almost archetypal figure regarded divorce as unthinkable not because marriage is "sacred" but because it is a contract, breaking of which even under the extremest provocation (in the novel, adultery) strikes at all organized society. Alternatively one might imagine a society based on the ruler-subject mode. Such a society, dominated by power relationships, is the ideal type to which totalitarian states, primitive "status" societies (in Sir Henry Maine's term, or "closed" in Karl Popper's), and military organizations approximate.

Following a shift in the dominant mode of transaction—from, say, the buyer-seller to the ruler-subject pattern, as has occurred in the United States—the entire culture must adjust itself to the new pattern. Syntactic forces will foster sympathetic changes in values, beliefs, and attitudes. Law must change too. The task of diachronic analysis, as it is called in anthropology, is to follow through the kinds of shifts that movement from one dominant mode to another induces in the functioning of a society's institutions. Thus a society's syntax, conceived as centered on one dominant mode of social transaction, provides a framework both for comparative analysis of societies and for dynamic analysis of changes within that society—changes which may lead to shifts from one dominant mode to another.

While societies manifest what William Graham Sumner

in *Folkways* (1906) called the "strain toward consistency"
—toward integration and coherence—such consistency is
never complete, at least not if the society is dynamic, adap-
tive, "alive." An effective syntax is likely to be influenced by
ideas from other cultures, as in the diffusionist model of
anthropology. Syntax can also be upset by technological developments, demographic changes, and the discovery of
new resources—all of which loom large in United States
history. Law can advance or retard adjustment. The Supreme Court in the 1950's and 1960's gained a reputation
as a precipitator of social change. But in the long term its
effect has been retardative, even reactionary. The question
is, why?

No society can remake its culture out of whole cloth in response to pressures for change. The same may be said me-
tonymously of most social institutions, including *a fortiori*
the Supreme Court. The Court is not merely a surrogate of
culture, but, like culture, is limited in its ability to respond
to change. It must work from within a received budget of
legal and social concepts. The traditional activity of constitutional interpretation is best described in the essentially
untranslatable French word *bricolage*. *Bricolage* is a process of fabricating "make-do" solutions to problems as they
arise, using a limited and often severely limiting store of
doctrines, materials, and tools—the way a household
handyman must respond to a novel "fix-it" task, relying only
on his ingenuity and a small kit bag of mending tools. The
source of the doctrines and exegetical tools employed by
constitutional judges is the society's "political culture." The
irony is that broader cultural influences are not themselves
always broadening in their effect on the law, but rather,
through the constraints of *bricolage*, are often limiting.

Constitutional *bricolage*, the art of judges, reflects the
larger process by which a society tries to maintain its syntax—its consistency and identity over time—by selecting responses to problems as they arise from a limited cultural
reserve. The problems that have confronted American

society have been diverse—securing private-property rights, stimulating economic growth in the post–Civil War period, responding to a crippling Depression, coping with violent and polarizing dissent. Yet juridical response to these challenges, because it is rooted in a single reserve of constitutional doctrine centered on the buyer-seller mode, has displayed a remarkable homogeneity—and, some would say, often an equally noteworthy lack of pertinence and imagination.

Metaphors, rules, and doctrines suited to dominance of the buyer-seller mode have continued to supply the interpretive needs of America's judicial *bricoleurs*, even as fundamental changes have occurred in society's network of relationships. Increasingly, allocations are determined by the relative power of individuals and groups—that is, by ruler-subject transactions—rather than through contractual exchanges of rights and obligations among equal buyers and sellers. The resulting strain to bring the rubrics of public law into line with the realities of society has posed the most wearing, persistent challenge to America's constitutional tradition.

Dominance of the buyer-seller mode does not necessarily produce a regime of indefeasible "rights," as federalist judges in their regard for sanctity of contract implied. Government can, by judiciously restricting individual freedom, help produce an environment in which the majority actually enjoys increased safety and opportunity. A society without the capacity to use power on its members' behalf might see a proliferation of privately imposed servitudes, not a maximization of freedom. Thus during the heyday of laissez-faire, from 1875 or so until the mid-1930's, the power of industry over material, job, and capital markets delivered High Capitalism from unreliable or over-costly labor and unhedgeable economic risks. Uncritical judicial acceptance of the efficacy and morality of "sanctity of contract," originally an agent of social integration, became disintegrative. The theme of rich versus poor was hardly a new one. But

the relatively small number of the rich, their apparent
heedlessness of growing numbers of the poor, and the
classes' increasingly polarized political values, were unprecedented. Free exchange among putative equals became less and less descriptive of Guilded Age America.

⌈The New Deal aimed at reducing the *de facto* servitudes
in which the *de jure* liberties of laissez-faire had enmeshed
a large part of the population⌋ Government would help secure personal and social rights by freeing individuals from
want, vicissitude, and arbitrary control from whatever
source—including the power of private employers. Yet not-
withstanding the Supreme Court's eventual ratification of
the New Deal under threat of F.D.R.'s Court-Packing plan,
the justices' subsequent preoccupation with personal freedoms continued in the older judicial tradition—the tradition of constitutional *bricolage*, in which new problems
were confronted by a constraining budget of doctrines originally evolved to moderate buyer-seller transactions.

⌈What is needed is a new syntax in which public law recognizes the realities of inequitable and often repressive
power—recognizes them and acts in order to change them.
New departures in the areas of free speech and criminal
justice evidence such a determination. Nevertheless, polarization is increasing. What syntax exists becomes more and
more exclusively "political" in the generic sense. Power—
often the power of the nightstick—rather than shared
norms, attitudes, and beliefs bind groups one to another,
often in relationships of exploitation and tension.⌋

Law, if not a manifestation of political culture at a suffi-
ciently general level to represent most of society's needs,
can become an active force for disintegration. This happened in the laissez-faire era. And history seems to be re-
peating itself today. Thus the question of syntax becomes
an issue of dominant interest in the 1970's. Perhaps too, consideration of the lag caused by continued judicial fealty to
a jurisprudence rooted in the buyer-seller mode at a time

when ruler-subject relationships are becoming dominant will give new perspective to the challenge of a realistic jurisprudence. No less important are the constraints of *bricolage*. At both the constitutional and the cultural levels, *bricolage* limits the speed and completeness with which society can respond to threats of division, factionalism, and polarization.

CHAPTER I

THE SYNTACTIC APPROACH AND THE PRIMACY OF FORM

THE FOLLOWING sentences illustrate two patterns. There is a vertical or *paradigmatic* pattern, showing the correct inflections of words depending on tense, number, and so forth; and a horizontal or *syntactic* pattern, following the rules governing combination of words to form correct sentences:

The mouse	will have eaten	the cheese.
Mice	will have eaten	the cheese.
The mouse	will eat	the cheese.
Mice	will eat	the cheese.
The mouse	has eaten	the cheese.
Mice	have eaten	the cheese.
The mouse	ate	the cheese.
Mice	ate	the cheese.

Because culture reflects language, just as language mirrors culture, we might extend these patterns to a particular aspect of U. S. political culture, public law. American constitutional development could then be viewed as having both paradigmatic and syntactic aspects.

[1]

The Syntactic Approach Goes beyond Case Law, Emphasizing Interactions between, and Integration of, Law and Political Culture

Scholars of the American Constitution have traditionally stressed the paradigmatic aspects of their subject. The pedagogy of constitutional law is characteristically organized around substantive areas: Commerce, Due Process, or Freedom of Speech, Press, and Religion. The central doctrines in each area change over time, just as the verb in a sentence inflects as it moves through the tenses. Analysis of these changes, based on study of Supreme Court opinions, yields historical paradigms. Such paradigms are by the conventional view the objects of constitutional inquiry.

Let us consider for a moment the chief limitation of the paradigmatic approach. Case law incompletely, and hence inaccurately, represents the grounding of constitutional law in the political culture of which law is an integral and integrated part.

The limits of the American Constitution are not necessarily, and surely not exclusively, determined by specific case decisions. Lagging progress in school integration, for example, long after the Supreme Court's 1954 decree that desegregation was to proceed with "all deliberate speed,"[1] suggests that one must look far beyond the decisions to learn what behavioral rules really bind individuals. Similar records of lagging compliance are to be found in the areas of school prayer and criminal procedure.[2]

Case law is not only frequently ineffective. It is often silent, even with respect to matters of fundamental public import. Many issues are "constitutional" in that they pose questions of the legitimacy of certain exercises of public power, yet do not lend themselves to litigation as justiciable conflicts. Such issues—so-called "political questions" are salient examples—fail what Justice Robert Jackson has characterized as "perhaps the most significant and least comprehended limitation upon the judicial power."[3] Sometimes, too, cases which would otherwise be justiciable are never pressed in court, either for lack of money or for fear that the decision will set an unfavorable precedent.

There frequently results a time-lapse between a legislative or executive exertion of power—the first actual influ-

[1] *Brown* v. *Board*, 349 U.S. 294, 301 (1955).

[2] See Robert Coles, *Children of Crisis* (Boston, 1964); note also, "Implementation of Desegregation by the Lower Courts," *Harvard Law Rev.*, 71 (January 1958), 486; Frank Sorauf, "Zorach v. Clauson: The Impact of a Supreme Court Decision," *Amer. Pol. Sci. Rev.*, 53 (September 1959), 777; Abraham S. Blumberg, *Criminal Justice* (Quadrangle, Chicago, 1967), pp. 21-32 and passim.

[3] Robert H. Jackson, *The Supreme Court in the American System of Government* (Cambridge, Mass., 1955), p. 11.

encing of behavior—and judicial decision in a case testing the legality of the act. That the courts are thus sometimes silent can hardly mean that the Constitution itself is in some sort of suspension pending judicial utterance. On the contrary, the sources of law lie not in cases, but in society's values and functional needs, embodied in its political culture. Judicial decisions themselves gain force from the fact that they mirror underlying cultural norms. These norms continue to manifest themselves under various forms. Hence they continue authoritatively to influence behavior, even in the absence of *or sometimes in spite of* judicial decisions.

Let us consider, therefore, an alternative to the paradigmatic approach, one better calculated to point up the relationship between law and culture. Syntactic analysis may be thought of as a "horizontal" study of the way various substantive areas fit together at a given time, like words in a sentence, to form a meaningful whole.

"Law," "culture," and "society," together with any sub-elements of these broad categories, impose restrictions on one another just as a plural noun for the subject of a sentence restricts, by the rules of syntax, the form that the verb may take. If the values actually served by law are widely inconsistent with cultural norms, either the law will fall into *to a degree* disrespect (as under Prohibition), or the culture will be forced at enormous pains into new patterns of value, attitude, and belief (as in Japan under the American occupation after World War II). Or else both law and culture will be in for hard mutual adjustment (as in the South, faced with integration).

Like Versailles mirrors, law, culture, and society reflect one another. Yet they reflect one another obliquely: never on a one-to-one basis, and rarely completely or perfectly. How perfect a reflection is possible—or desirable? How imperfect a reflection is tolerable? The syntactic approach provokes such questions. When considering the subject syntactically, we are cued to problems which result when one paradigm or line of constitutional development moves at a different pace or in a different direction from a second paradigm with which the first must articulate. Just as in the "mouse ate the cheese" example, syntax shifts with paradigm. Nouns must inflect along with the verbs. What society *is* must be consistent with what it tries to *do.*

[2]

Political Culture Expresses Itself Through Various Forms, One of which Is Law; This Reflection of a Deeper Unity Gives Coherence and Continuity to Constitutional Interpretation

The syntactic approach emphasizes form—specifically, the forms in which the various aspects of a coherent culture reflect themselves in one another. The syntactic approach furnishes a principle of continuity in U.S. constitutional interpretation, one transcending the apparent discontinuities in the historical paradigms occasioned by reversals in substantive doctrine. Such discontinuities are accounted for syntactically as attempts to restore coherence in the political culture by bringing various areas of substantive doctrine into harmony with one another through judicial decision, after earlier shifts in society's values or needs have triggered an adjustment in some aspect of the pre-existing social syntax. *Discontinuities are modifications of one or more paradigms to achieve syntax.*

There can be no better example or harder test of this thesis than the apparent discontinuity dividing constitutional history into the two eras, before and after 1937. A contemporary observer might have thought that the Supreme Court's about-face in 1937, sustaining the New Deal in defiance of the case-law precedents, would have laid to rest controversy over alleged special access by judges to special knowledge. "Courts are mere instruments of the law and can will nothing," Marshall had written in 1824.[4] Yet the reversals of 1937 demonstrated that judges are political actors sensitive to political pressures, not impassive oracles of an inner harmony and higher majesty—The Law.

[4] *Osborne* v. *Bank*, 9. Wheat. 738, 866.

A new Court carried on. But so, to an amazing extent, did the old fiction. More than twenty years after the New Deal shifts, Learned Hand observed that judges, when voiding legislation, "do not, indeed may not say that, taking all things into consideration, the legislator's solution is too strong for the judicial stomach. On the contrary, they wrap their veto in a protective veil of adjectives such as 'arbitrary,' 'artificial,' 'normal,' 'reasonable,' 'inherent,' 'fundamental,' or 'essential,' whose office usually, though quite innocently, is to disguise what they are doing and impute it to a derivation far more impressive than their personal preferences, which are all that in fact lie behind the decision."[5] Hand's words underscore the primacy of form in constitutional adjudication.

To give yet another example, in 1936 Justice Owen Roberts published his famed essay in judicial obscurantism:[6]

When an act of Congress is appropriately challenged [the Supreme Court] has only one duty—to lay the article of the Constitution which is invoked beside the statute which is challenged and to decide whether the latter squares with the former. . . . This court neither approves nor condemns any legislative policy. Its delicate and difficult office is to ascertain and declare whether the legislation is in accordance with, or in contravention of, the provisions of the Constitution; and, having done that, its duty ends.

Two decades later, in an opinion for the Court, Chief Justice Warren returned to the same, and some had thought discredited, measuring-rod theory, arguing that constitutional interpretation "requires the exercise of judgment, not the reliance on personal preferences. Courts must not consider the wisdom of statutes but neither can they sanction as being merely unwise that which the Constitution forbids."[7]

[5] Learned Hand, *The Bill of Rights* (Cambridge, Mass., 1958), p. 70.
[6] *U.S.* v. *Butler*, 297 U.S. 1, 62-63.
[7] *Trop* v. *Dulles*, 356 U.S. 86, 103 (1957).

Judicial obscurantism—as a positive technique of, rather than merely an exasperating limitation on, the jurist's art— was not simply a by-product of dominant Court views in the pre-1937 era. The tendency to screen motivations with protestations of a higher compelling objectivity seems inherent in the judicial process. In this tendency we find the sought-for continuity, an otherwise absent consistency to Court history, which links by a common factor—fealty to the "right" forms—the periods before and after 1937, despite reversals in substantive doctrine. This book presents an interpretation of Supreme Court history, stressing three related aspects of judicial form, which broadly correspond to the validation, generation, and significance of form as elements of the political culture underlying court decisions.

[3]

Form Both Limits Judicial Freedom and Legitimizes Decisions by Prescribing The Terms in which Decisions Must Be Cast and the Process Used to Reach Them

There exist definite forms in which Court decisions are, and perhaps must be, cast if they are to be received as valid resolutions of disputes. Judges, by the nature of their institution and calling as well as by the proclivities of the "legal mind," work within an inherited tradition. This tradition both draws strength from and itself reinforces the primacy of form in adjudication.

The judicial tradition is keyed to achieve continuity, as indeed is any tradition. A main way of achieving continuity is to develop standard forms into which behavior (including verbal behavior) must be fitted. The very fact that they are standard tends to make the use of such forms recurrent. Their recurrence helps validate them as traditional, as acceptable, as "the right way." Therefore, a court functions more effectively and easily if its rulings—regardless of their substantive purport, regardless of the logical or psychological processes employed in reaching them—are presented in the form of a more or less skillful combination and permutation of the received standard elements. Form, so used, may of course control the substance of decisions, even to the point of making the court "dysfunctional" in its impact on society. This possibility will be dealt with at length in the following pages.

Judicial reliance on received forms—the talismans of the law—is suggested in the term "constitutional *bricolage.*" This term follows the French word (introduced into social science literature by Claude Levi-Strauss)[8] for a do-it-your-self handyman who must solve problems using only a limited, previously provided resource of tools and a developed flair for putting these resources to unanticipated, often difficult uses.

Consider a recent instance of constitutional *bricolage.* The Supreme Court's tendency to rely on received forms goes far to explain the rise (from 1920 till about 1945) and decline (1945 to 1950) of "clear and present danger" as a test of government action touching speech. Edward S. Corwin has shown that Holmes and Brandeis, in a string of dissents during the 1920's developed this test from a felicitous phrase first penned by Holmes apparently without awareness of its potentiality to be used as anything more than a felicitous phrase.[9] Form *became* substance.

The idea itself derived, ironically enough, not from the law of civil liberties but from an earlier Holmes opinion in a labor case, *Gompers* v. *Buck Stove*, sustaining punishment for leaders of a secondary boycott on the ground that their action illegally burdened interstate commerce.[10] Interpretation of the First Amendment's free-speech guarantee has proceeded almost as a running gloss on "clear and present danger"—from the Holmes-Brandeis development of a constitutional catchword, through its invocation, sometimes uncritically, to support libertarian holdings in the late 1930's and early 1940's,[11] to its eclipse by Learned Hand's "clear and probable danger" test in the *Dennis* case (1951).

[8] Claude Levi-Strauss, *The Savage Mind* (Chicago, 1962, 1968), pp. 16ff.

[9] Edward S. Corwin, "Bowing Out 'Clear and Present Danger,'" *Notre Dame Lawyer*, 27 (Spring 1952), 325.

[10] 221 U.S. 418.

[11] *Herndon* v. *Lowry*, 301 U.S. 242 (1937); *Thornhill* v. *Alabama*, 310 U.S. 88 (1940); *Craig* v. *Harney* 331 U.S. 367 (1947).

But even here, continuity of form was paramount. The Supreme Court accepted Hand's phrase not as a new rule, but as a more precise statement of the original Holmes formulation.[12] The requirement to maintain accepted forms by couching pronouncements, to the extent feasible, in terms having prior lodgement in the constitutional tradition generalizes, in a psychological sense, the logical requirement of consistency with precedent. In constitutional *bricolage* we find a basic source of stability and continuity in American public law.

Decisions, to be valid, must be reached by procedures correct in form as well as explicated in the accepted, authoritative idiom. Indeed, the centrality of process in American jurisprudence, with its emphasis on fair and complete procedures to safeguard all parties' rights, reflects and articulates with other aspects of U.S. society. It well illustrates the syntactic principle.

The high value placed on procedural regularity reflects a society marked by substantial diversity of interests, but one in which an acculturated sense of fair play requires that all parties interested in a controversy have a role in determining its outcome. Procedure is thus designed to insure access to decision-making and a fair hearing all round. But the right to be heard is not a guarantee that one will be listened to, and substance may be the casualty of form. So does it work in practice. In administrative law, for example, provision for intervention in cases even by parties with remote interests in a dispute has contributed to a backlog in U.S. regulatory agencies neither less shocking nor more conducive to smooth government than the backlogs on criminal court dockets—this in a system where "justice delayed is justice denied."

The idea of criminal justice as a special branch of law proceeds from, and implements, the thesis that the public itself must be represented in the process that will be used to make good the damage done in an alleged crime. Some basic advances in Anglo-American law illustrate this theme:

[12] 341 U.S. 494, 510, Chief Justice Vinson citing 183 F. 2d 212.

the elimination of "outlawry," for instance, and the prohibition of conflict settlement by duel or vendetta. Such practices left resolution of disputes to private action, often by means and with results invidious to the public weal. Criminal law asserts that the public is always interested in any matter defined as "criminal." Indeed, nothing less than the existence of a public concern provides the ground for defining a given act as a crime.

American courts work not by haruspication, divine intervention, or shamanism. Decisions resolving conflicts issue not from "trial by ordeal" but from publicly ascertainable, reproducible, and reviewable procedures for presentation and weighing of evidence. Power rationalized is not always power legitimized, but power to be legitimized should be rationalized—that is, exerted only under general legal rubrics prescribing the circumstances under which sanctions for prohibited behavior may be applied. In few respects does American law more clearly or thoroughly reflect the American political culture than in this strain toward rationalization.

Finally, procedure is emphasized because fairness, in and of itself, stands high among American values. The importance of "fair play" in the Anglo-American heritage tends to tip the legal system in favor of procedure—the forms that must be observed in reaching decisions—over substance. Nor is it a coincidence that America's professional mechanics of procedure, lawyers, reserve their most eloquent raptures for celebrations of process. Justice Robert Jackson once wrote:[13]

Only the untaught layman or the charlatan lawyer can answer that procedures matter not. Procedural fairness and regularity are of the indispensable essence of liberty. Severe substantive laws can be endured if they are fairly and impartially applied. Indeed, if put to the choice one might well prefer to live under Soviet substantive law applied in good faith by our common-law procedures than

[13] *Shaughnessy* v. *U.S.*, 345 U.S. 206, 224 (1953).

under our substantive law enforced by Soviet procedural practices.

Veneration of process is a symptom of legalism, discussed in Chapter IV. The deeper sources of legalism in American political culture, no less than its impact on American politics, are main subjects of the analysis that follows.

[4]
Court Decisions are Often Grounded in "Resolving Formulas" Embodying Socially Approved Solutions for Recurrent Types of Conflict

Judicial holdings usually follow from a formula embodying a socially approved solution to a whole class of conflicts. Thus judicial decision-making is not merely a process of totting up positive and negative affects under the stimulus of a given set of facts. It involves logical effort to establish the class of accepted formulas under which a case is to be brought.

Courts, like societies at large—indeed, like any organism or organization—must husband energies. Judges face crowded dockets, hurried opinion schedules. They must economize their psychic and intellectual resources, an end to which the habit of *bricolage* makes an obvious contribution.

Another obvious way to economize energies for productive uses (i.e., for the creation of new values) as distinct from merely restorative uses (i.e., repairing past omissions or errors), is by minimizing conflicts in a society before they happen. To this end, society makes rules. When rules fail to prevent conflict, a need emerges to restore economically any resulting rent in the social fabric. This need is met by reference to appropriate broad categories of usage or custom, to law, or to ethical, social, or political theory which suggest a line of resolution—a "resolving formula."

The categories from which resolving formulas derive frequently correspond to certain basic modes of social relationship. Formulas applicable to the relationship of buyer to seller, as will be shown, dominated American constitutional law down through 1937. For each mode of social transaction, then, rules are devised prescribing the rights and duties of the parties to a relationship. Conflict results from a perceived failure by one party to discharge his duties or, which is the same thing, to respect the other's rights. Court cases arise from conflicts. It follows that court decisions are sensitive to the judges' determination of the transactional mode from which a given instance of conflict-generating behavior arises, a determination on which resolving formulas applicable to the case depend.

An approach to constitutional interpretation dealing with the sensitivity of decisions to such formulas should specify mechanisms which permit the judge to function as a surrogate for the culture of which such resolving formulas are a part. Such a link between court and culture, it is also clear, is simultaneously the means whereby judges may contribute toward the development of a working syntax by resolving conflicts in a manner consistent with shared norms, attitudes, and beliefs. The judicial "mental set" can furnish such a link.

A mental set may be thought of as a culturally developed (learned rather than inborn) intellectual screen through which an individual habitually filters ideas and data.[14] The selection helps insure that behavior will be consistent with whatever basic values are served by the set, which is "programmed" to eliminate stimuli that might dispose the individual to inconsistent behavior. Such programming is done through the acculturation or socialization process. *Hence the mental set, a product of one's culture, helps keep behavior (physical or intellectual) consistent with culture; and development of an effective syntax is the result of effective acculturation and socialization.*

Consider the work of T. W. Adorno and his associates, published in *The Authoritarian Personality*. Adorno demonstrated a "close correspondence in the type of approach

[14] See in this connection Klaus Knorr, "Failures in National Intelligence Estimates," *World Politics*, 16 (April 1964), 455, esp. 457.

and outlook a subject is likely to have in a great variety of areas, ranging from the most intimate features of family and sex adjustment through relationships to other people in general, to religion and to social and political philosophy." An authoritarian mental set predisposes certain individuals to consistent, more or less predictable, reactions in response to a wide range of stimuli:[15]

> A basically hierarchical, authoritarian exploitive parent-child relationship is apt to carry over into a power-oriented, exploitively dependent attitude toward one's sex partner and one's God and may well culminate in a political philosophy and social outlook which has no room for anything but a desperate clinging to whatever appears to be strong and a disdainful rejection of whatever is relegated to the bottom.

The mental-set concept suggests how consistent patterns of value, attitude, and belief are transmitted over time —behavior by authoritarian parents stimulating the development of authoritarian personalities in their children, and so forth. Such intergenerational transmission of traits relates paradigm to syntax. The mental set thus becomes a mechanism for integrating individuals' norms, attitudes, and beliefs into coherent cultural patterns, and in turn for reproducing dominant cultural traits in individuals.

The mental set facilitates economy. A culture that produces, and a society that accredits, decision-makers disposed to regarding problems as arising from buyer-seller transactions will waste little energy debating which kind of resolving rules should be applied. Formulas developed for the buyer-seller mode will automatically present themselves. Almost as automatically, they will be invoked by judges as rules of law. As we shall see in Chapter vi, during the nineteenth and early twentieth centuries, America's mercantile culture helped staff the Supreme Court with judges possessing just such a mental set. We shall see too

[15] T. W. Adorno, *et al.*, *The Authoritarian Personality* (New York, 1950), p. 971.

with what economy and power this notion helps us interpret both the trend of constitutional interpretation during the Gilded Age and the problems for the Court resulting therefrom in the 1930's.

Much of the following analysis, then, will concern the process whereby formulations of conflict situations attain the status of mental sets, tending thence to become decisive qua formulas of specific court cases. Such mental sets, and the formula jurisprudence they imported into the judicial process, contributed as much as did logical analysis of precedents toward such thematic coherence as the Supreme Court's decisional paradigms achieved.

[5]

In Social Morphological Terms, Courts Function as Surrogates of the Political Culture, and Decisions Are but Formal Enunciations of Basic Norms

Form may finally be treated from the viewpoint of social morphology, and the place of judicial opinions in society's overall structure of norms, beliefs, and attitudes may be considered.

Learned Hand charged that constitutional decisions often reflect judges' personal preferences. Yet frequently such personal preferences are themselves but mediating, intervening variables. The mental-set concept suggests that these preferences both link decisions to, and screen them from, a more basic energizing force. Judges' preferences themselves result from an acculturation and socialization process; judges serve, even if unwittingly, as surrogates of their ambient political culture. A constitutional decision is an attempt to represent society's shared norms, beliefs, and attitudes in more official and dignified form, under the special rubric of "law."

Not every court ruling mirrors some broader principle, or one that has universal acceptance. "Culture" commands varying degrees of fealty across society. Often what is decisive is the accepted norm of the group in society that holds dominant power. In the United States lawyers are repre-

sented in that group quite disproportionately to their numbers. Judges' mental sets reflect something different from,
and more than, the lowest common denominator of shared
norms, attitudes, and beliefs in the society in which the
Court operates. Judges are specially recruited. Moreover,
judges and lawyers have an artificial, technical culture of
their own making. The life of professional legalism is ab-
stracted, literally as well as figuratively, from the lay concerns and common sense wisdoms that bulk large in "culture" as the term is usually employed. Yet it seems reasonable to hypothesize an at least long-run tendency toward
convergence of judicial reasoning with society's values and
needs, if only because of society's ability to discipline judges
in advance through acculturation and socialization.

Thus every society must generate means to insure adequate socialization of its members, or at least of the vast
majority of its members, in what might be termed its Law
of Rules. Law in the formal sense is rooted in and reflects
these rules.

Let us consider a contemporary example. Most Americans first learn certain important social rules in childhood
games. The sociologist Omar K. Moore[16] has argued that
sandlot games are not mere pastimes, but socializing vehicles to teach children the importance of rules. One of the
first rules is that of fair play—the strong must not take undue advantage of the weak, or the more knowledgeable of
information denied his adversary.

For a game to serve its purpose, it must be fair. If the
rules are broken, the game is not fair. Generalizing from the
attitudes and values—the mental sets—inculcated by youth-
ful training in fair play, one may say there exists a normative framework, applicable to most adversary situations,
which makes adjustments in the relative advantages of both
parties in order to offset disparities in weight, experience,

---

[16] Omar K. Moore and A. R. Anderson, "Some Puzzling Aspects of
Social Interaction," in *Mathematical Models in Small Group Processes*
ed., J. Crawford, H. Solomon, and P. Suppes (Stanford, Calif., 1962),
pp. 232-249.

age, or ability (handicaps in golf and bowling, for example, and fighting with one hand tied). Margaret Mead has commented on the pervasiveness of the fair-play rule in her study of American national character, *And Keep Your Powder Dry*:[17]

> Fair play means certain definite things. It means "obeying the rules," and the rules are thought of as a device for keeping people from bullying or taking unfair advantage of the other person. One's character is defined by the way in which the rules are embodied in one's behavior—and "That's not cricket" may be applied to making love to the wife of a man who is in a weaker tradition than one's self.

Rules of fair play, initially encountered in the common law of backyards and playgrounds, thus become a guide for behavior in other spheres. Law in the formal sense, by giving the fair-play rule a special status in society's official values, replicates a more basic structure or prescribed form of social interaction. *Through the achievement of such morphological parallelisms among the various aspects of society, syntax is achieved, and the society itself brought to functional effectiveness.*

The fair-play norm finds reflection in, for example, the "fair-trial rule."[18] Supreme Court decisions widening the rights to legal counsel of indigent and ignorant accused persons[19] are animated by a desire to insure equity in the adversary confrontation of state and lone citizen. Revolutionary constitutional decisions in the racial field evidence a broad federal commitment to positive action insuring equality in opportunity.

The fair-play rule is seen in the authority of the Federal Trade Commission to protect consumers from false ad-

[17] New York, 1942, 1965, p. 143.
[18] See summary of cases in A. T. Mason and W. M. Beaney, *American Constitutional Law* (Englewood Cliffs, N.J., 1968), pp. 444ff.
[19] Esp. *Gideon* v. *Wainwright*, 373 U.S. 335 (1963); *Escobedo* v. *Illinois*, 378 U.S. 478 (1964); *Miranda* v. *Arizona*, 384 U.S. 436 (1966).

vertising; in the principle—however much observed in the breach—which limits political campaign expenses and partisan activity by civil servants, lest the wealthy or the "in" party gain an undue advantage; in the prohibition against Wall Street insiders' taking advantage of privileged stock market information. Indeed, the constitutional revolution of 1937 itself represented a kind of judicial recognition of fair play as the guiding norm in the economic sphere, in that the Court's liberal holdings helped adjust an inequitable balance of power in American society in favor of the previously disadvantaged.

As in the areas of criminal justice, racial equality, regulatory law and economic power, so too in the field of substantive civil liberties. In *Palko* v. *Connecticut* (1937), long after the Court had settled that the "liberty" protected by the Fourteenth Amendment included certain substantive freedoms of the First Amendment, Justice Benjamin Cardozo reaffirmed for an eight-man majority that the Bill of Rights had not been incorporated wholesale in the Fourteenth Amendment. After surveying the relevant "incorporation" cases, Cardozo asserted:[20]

> There emerges the perception of a rationalizing principle which gives to discrete instances a proper order and coherence. The right to trial by jury and the immunity from prosecution except as the result of an indictment may have value and importance. Even so, they are not of the very essence of a scheme of ordered liberty. To abolish them is not to violate a "principle of justice so rooted in the traditions and conscience of our people as to be ranked as fundamental. . . ."
> We reach a different plane of social and moral values when we pass to the privileges and immunities that have been taken over from the earlier articles of the Federal Bill of Rights and brought within the Fourteenth Amendment by a process of absorption. These in their origin were effective against the federal government alone. If

[20] 302 U.S. 319, 325-326.

the Fourteenth Amendment has absorbed them, the process of absorption has had its source in the belief that neither liberty nor justice would exist if they were sacrificed.

Cardozo's appeal was not to the constitutional tradition in any narrow sense, nor to the body of rules on constitutional civil liberties considered as *sui generis* or self-contained. Cardozo rather invoked the constitutional tradition as a reflection of the political culture of which it is a part. This, we shall see, has been the general pattern and form of constitutional argumentation—from Chancellor Kent's and Joseph Story's arguments on behalf of private property in the early national era, to Oliver Wendell Holmes' early twentieth-century dissents against judicial treatment of property as sacrosanct. This same fact points to the approach to be used in the following analysis.

CHAPTER II

THE LAW
OF RULES

In 1899, Holmes asserted: "It is perfectly proper to regard and study the law simply as a great anthropological document . . . as an exercise in the morphology and transformation of human ideas."[1] Such an approach requires more than transference to modern legal scholarship of illuminating perspectives from reports on savage, primitive, or otherwise exotic peoples. It requires treatment of law as an institution in terms of its social function among complementary institutions performing other functions, and all contributing to a more or less coherent whole.

Even a preliminary attempt at such an essay presupposes: (1) a theory of the relationship between the allocation of values in a society on the one hand and the norms which moderate conflict and reduce inefficiencies in that allocative process on the other; and (2) a theory of the reasons and means whereby certain rules are given broader, coercive backing as "laws" by society as a whole. Chapters II–IV attempt to provide the required theoretical framework.

[1]

Regularized Social Transactions Generate Repetitive Modes of Behavior, Certain of which Become Dominant and Characteristic Features in a Given Society

"Society" implies, at minimum, satisfaction of two conditions: that there be more than one individual, and that these individuals somehow interact with one another. Some sociologists and anthropologists require that more stringent requirements be satisfied before they will consider a given aggregate of people to be a society—for example, that the interaction patterns be regularized or "institutionalized"; or that the members share a common awareness of partici-

---

[1] O. W. Holmes, Jr., "Law in Science and Science in Law," *Harvard Law Rev.*, 12 (February 1899), 443, 444.

pation in a group distinguished from all other groups by common background, ancestry, goals, usages, or values. Robert Redfield's definition is to this effect: "A society is people feeling solidarity with one another."[2] But these characteristics are usually consequences of the conditions of plurality and interaction, for reasons to be considered in this chapter. The following analysis therefore proceeds from a concept of society limited to the two requirements given above.

That individuals (or organized groups, such as business firms or charitable foundations composed ultimately of individuals) interact implies the existence not only of the social actors themselves, but also of objects of their interactions. Thus society suggests a network of contacts as a result of which values of all sorts pass from one individual to another. The figure is that of a continuous flow of values, or advantages and disadvantages, among society's members, resulting from a series of discrete transactions by each individual. The term "value" will be used in a neutral sense, so as not to prejudge whether an individual attaches a positive or a negative valence to a given transaction.

The idea that a transaction always results in some reallocation of values (which may include the creation or destruction of values) may be expressed symbolically:

$$\text{Transaction} \rightarrow \text{Allocation}$$

Thus the concept of society in this analysis recalls David Easton's definition of politics as the "authoritative allocation of values."[3] Both society and politics have to do with allocations of advantages and disadvantages. Indeed, the allocation at any time is largely the cumulative result of past interactions, each of which in its turn affected, however slightly, the prior state of the society. What converts society into a politically organized body is the introduction or recognition of an agency (usually called government)

[2] Robert Redfield, "How Human Society Operates," in *Man, Culture and Society,* ed. Harry Shapiro (New York, 1960), p. 346.

[3] David Easton, *The Political System* (New York, 1963), p. 129.

endowed by power or by some philosophy of "right"—or most frequently by a combination of the two—with the ability authoritatively to influence allocations.

There are four modes of social transaction, that is, four ways to achieve a flow of value from one individual (or group) to another. As indicated in Table I, each mode is definable by a dyadic relationship; each occurs in a characteristic "space"—as the buyer-seller transaction, for example, may commonly be said to occur in a "market"; and each has a characteristic interpersonal operation.

Table I. *Modes of Social Interaction*

Transactional Category	Characteristics	
	"Space"	Operation
1. Buyer-Seller	Markets	Exchange
2. Ruler-Subject	Domains	Control
3. Donor-Donee	Communes	Gift
4. Patron-Protégé	Neighborhoods	Parasitism

In buyer-seller transactions, values are exchanged by achieving an equation between supply and demand. A price is paid by one party, in money or in kind; some value is provided by the second party in return. Since the second actor gives up the value in order to get the price, the flow is two-way. Three aspects of exchange bear special attention: the defining characteristics of the transaction; the potential of exchange as an organizing principle of society; and the generality of the buyer-seller concept.

There are two distinguishing marks in any buyer-seller transaction. First, mutuality: each party desires the exchange. In the terminology of contract law, there must exist a "meeting of the minds" between parties before a trade can be validly agreed to. In the economist's calculus of gains and costs, each must feel he gets more out of the deal than it costs him to conclude it. Second, the buyer-seller mode implies reciprocity. Each actor gives the other something of value (of value to the other, that is) in exchange for something desired in return. Again in legal parlance, it is required that "consideration pass" for the contract or exchange to be (legally) valid or (analytically) a genuine instance of a buyer-seller transaction, thus excluding acquisition of goods by means of gift, in which there is no two-way flow. Reciprocity, and often also mutuality, further excludes acquisition through patronage or parasitism, in which one individual takes free advantage of another's efforts.

The buyer-seller concept as used in these pages is not limited to the kinds of exchanges on which the discipline of economics focuses, that is, exchanges mainly of scarce physical goods in commodity, money, or stock markets. The concept is used more generally, to suggest any social situation whose dominant characteristic is exchange or the reallocation of values on some *quid pro quo* basis. Thus the conditions of the buyer-seller mode are satisfied in many legal agreements, especially those covered by actual or implied contract. They are often satisfied in politicians' "deals," in international agreements, and in labor–management bargains; and they underlie the patronage system. Exchange in this broad sense furnishes the activating idea behind the sexual division of labor. As such it plays a central role in the institution of marriage;[4] and the sexual ramifications of exchange go beyond wedlock too, to courtesanship and prostitution.

The generality, not to say downright ubiquity, of the buyer-seller relationship implies a like generality of social norms pertaining to exchange. The concept of exchange may be applied to the procedures for producing and distributing goods and services which tend in any society to become embedded in "noneconomic" aspects of social life. Systematic study of this tendency by Bronislaw Malinow-

[4] See Claude Levi-Strauss, "The Family," in *Man, Culture and Society*, ed., Harry Shapiro, pp. 269, 274.

ski furnished a turning point in scientific anthropology. Malinowski's reasoning is relevant to the argument of this book.

While on an extended stay in Melanesia during World War I, Malinowski observed that the inland natives of the Trobriand Islands have no natural supply of fish. Conversely, the coast-dwelling natives, though able and normally successful fishermen, had no easy source of vegetables. Therefore the coastal natives traded their surplus catch for the inlanders' vegetables, and vice versa—a natural response to a quite common economic problem. But the matter did not end as a simple problem in economic marketing. Much of the coastal natives' social, political, and religious life turned on elaborate feasts. Custom decreed that the food served at these ceremonies must include large quantities of—what else?—vegetables. By a similar inversion, inland natives emphasized their rare good, seafood, on social occasions. "Thus, to all other reasons of value of the respectively rarer food," Malinowski observed, "there is added an artificially, culturally created dependence of the two districts upon one another. . . . Each community has, therefore, a weapon for the enforcement of its rights: reciprocity."

Malinowski raised—rather too prominently, most students of society now agree—reciprocity to the status of a master explanatory variable. He used it not only to account for the success and smoothness of native economic relationships, but also to explain the sanctions underlying the force of law in Trobriand society. Indeed, Malinowski found in exchange the essential link among peoples in primitive society: "Thus every chain of reciprocity is made the more binding by being part and parcel of a whole system of mutualities."[5]

The generality of the exchange concept relates the theoretical development in this chapter to the point made in

[5] Bronislaw Malinowski, *Crime and Custom in Savage Society* (London, 1926), pp. 22-23.

Chapter I regarding primacy of form. To say that judges resolve disputes by reference to general principles is to say that they decide what rules or formulas apply to given facts. Such a determination follows from a prior and more fundamental judgment that the conflict belongs within one or another mode of transaction. The choice of applicable rules then follows almost automatically. To this central point we shall have reason to return again and again.

Ruler-subject transactions include all social interactions in which a relationship of super- and subordination between the parties decides the outcome. Implicit is a distinction of power, formal or informal, private or public. As with the concepts already introduced, the concept of power will be used very broadly. It may include use of positively valued inducements or seductions instead of negatively valued sanctions to achieve this mode's characteristic feature: control of the subject's behavior against his will. Of course, inducement is frequently also central to exchange. Whether a given inducement, if successful, represents an exercise of power or an element of exchange is an empirical question, turning on the subject's perception of the actual case rather than on an *a priori* distinction.

This point is doubly crucial to the interpretation of constitutional history to be presented in the following pages. The vagueness of the line between some power and some exchange situations suggests how the Supreme Court, by deciding labor and industrial relations cases under the free-exchange formula, was able in the nineteenth century to screen the development of an essentially exploitative economy in which power, not contract, actually dominated employer–employee relationships. The fact that power has positive as well as negative dimensions also goes to the heart of post-1930's controversies over the impact of the "service state" orientation of the federal government. This controversy was prompted by the charge that expanded public authority to provide conditional rewards, benefits, and welfare services vested in government an unwisely, and perhaps an unconstitutionally, increased potential coercive power.[6]

Society exerts power through sanctions against violation of group norms through public opinion, or more subtly, by educating people's "consciences" to do the enforcement job on society's behalf. Malinowski told of the Melanesian native Kima'i, who was driven to suicide after the community had pointed the finger of shame at him for an incestuous love affair and, worse, for flaunting the sin before his mistress's prior suitor.[7] Robert Coles' study of school integration, *Children of Crisis*, contains a Southern teacher's account of her physical loathing upon realizing that she had showered in the same room with a Negro fellow student at Columbia University:[8]

> . . . suddenly I saw that nigra woman. . . . It was as if I'd seen the Devil himself, or was about to face Judgement Day. . . . I thought of everything I could do at once, but I felt paralyzed. I felt like fainting, and vomiting, too; it was shock, like seasickness; it took hold of me all over and I wondered whether I was about to die.

Kima'i's self-inflicted punishment was to avoid public shame. The teacher's emotional pain, equally a form of punishment, resulted from a private revulsion against a situation of which she had been an utterly unwitting cause. In each case, the sanction was negative and physical. But in each, the efficient power energizing the sanction was psychological. The ruler was personal only in a most attenuated, diffuse sense, for even in the teacher's case, the real source of the sanction was Southern society at large, that had so effectively acculturated her in its prejudices.

The diffuse power of the cultural ambiance figures importantly in an analysis of the American constitutional tradition, which relies on citizens' emotional and quasi-

---

[6] See Charles Reich, "The New Property," *Yale Law Journal*, 73 (April 1964), 733.

[7] Malinowski, *Savage Society*, pp. 77-78.

[8] Robert Coles, *Children of Crisis* (Boston, 1964), p. 149.

religious reverence for the Constitution. The notion of public opinion as a shaper of institutions and determinant of behavior, long a staple of ethnographic studies of primitive societies,[9] accords with a long-standing thesis on American cultural history as well. De Tocqueville remarked on the power of public opinion,[10] and David Riesman's *The Lonely Crowd* (1950), William Whyte's *The Organization Man* (1956), and Vance Packard's *The Status Seekers* (1959) have pointed up the continuing relevance of de Tocqueville's observations.

In the donor-donee mode, values pass from one individual to another as gifts outright. This mode is dominant in most families: children benefit from provident actions by their parents—normally, without charge. Even Marx and Engels realized that in the absence of the state, and therefore without its ability to insure forcefully (however inequitably) a functional allocation of values, people would have to rely on some alternative mode. In place of power as the moving force, socialism would substitute the "commune" or true classless state. Donor-donee relationships would exclusively and uniformly characterize social transactions, as in the prescript, "To each according to his need, from each according to his ability." That values are given by donor to donee without compensation distinguishes this from the buyer-seller mode. That gifts are given freely distinguishes the donor-donee from the ruler-subject relationship.

Finally, there is the patron-protégé concept, most fully developed by economists, especially Paul Samuelson, William J. Baumol, and Mancur Olson, Jr.[11] Analysis of this

[9] See the survey of sources in Carl J. Friedrich and Morton Horwitz, "Some Thoughts on the Relation of Political Theory to Anthropology," *Amer. Pol. Sci. Rev.*, 62 (June 1968), 536, 537, esp. nn. 4-7.

[10] Alexis de Tocqueville, *Democracy in America*, trans. Henry Reeve (London, 1835), 2: 159-160.

[11] Paul Samuelson, "A Pure Theory of Public Expenditures," *Review of Economics and Statistics*, 37 (1955), 350; William J. Baumol, *Welfare Economics and the Theory of the State* (Cambridge, Mass., 1952); Mancur Olson, *The Logic of Collective Action* (New York, 1964).

mode starts from the idea of "externalities," or production by one person of any effect not confined to the producer himself. Thus the beekeeper produces an external economy, free pollinators, for everyone in the neighborhood who likes wild flowers. But conscientious bees obviously are an external *dis*economy for the formal gardener who prefers personally to plan and regulate his flowers' genetic lines.

A patron-protégé relationship develops whenever a good is produced or procured by one individual (the patron) in his own self-interest, and then other individuals (the protégés), merely by putting themselves in proximity to the patron, benefit from his actions. For example, a citizen who successfully sues a neighbor for keeping pigs acts as a patron to every other non-pig-lover in the neighborhood. These neighbors will profit by the abatement of the nuisance, just as he will, by an amount varying with the distance of their own houses from the offender's, and at no cost to themselves. In the "external diseconomy" case it works in the opposite way. If the protégé is unable to get out of the patron's neighborhood—conceived as an analytical and not necessarily a geographical space—he must suffer the consequences, though he did nothing to create the situation.

The patron-protégé concept has an important, albeit limited, place in the development of the thesis of this book; we shall encounter it in Chapter VI.

[2]

Regularized Modal Behavior Gives Rise to Institutions, the "Organs" of Society; Internal Modal Conflicts Furnish a Prime Source of Institutional Change

Transactions tend to become organized and regularized, often on a mass scale, and often in the form of "official" entities. In the behavioral sense, an institution is a regularized way of doing something. Organically, an institution is a structure of determinate persons functioning in a more or less predictable way and for a predictable purpose or purposes. This duality between the behavioral and the organic is familiar in social science. For example, it corresponds in

Talcott Parsons' action theory to the distinction between "institutions" and "collectivities."[12] Henceforth an institution, when meant in the organic sense, will simply be referred to as an Institution with initial capitalization.

As we have seen, society may be viewed as a network of transactions among persons. It may also be viewed as a structure of patterned behavior; and again, as a structure of Institutions to regularize and help harmonize into a coherent whole the normal, necessary transactions of a functioning civilization.

Exchange (the buyer-seller mode) and power (the ruler-subject mode) are in many respects substitutable ways of getting society's business transacted. For instance cotton, once picked by slaves, today is picked by contract laborers whose toil is exchanged for a price rather than extorted under the lash. The general principle of modal substitutability suggests that different societies will tend to enlarge reliance on one mode or another, depending on existing norms and available technologies. One mode will tend over time to become comparatively more advantageous, and will thus become the typical solution to that society's allocative problem. A social syntax will then develop around the dominant mode.

Societies might be characterized by their dominant transactional tendencies, in the way that Malinowski characterized Trobriand society as exchange-dominated in many aspects—legal-political, ceremonial, and social as well as economic. Much of Western, and especially Anglo-American, social structure is a network of institutions, customs, and attitudes conducive to market exchange. On this thesis the buyer-seller model also dominates American society.

In contrast are totalitarian systems, in which ruler-subject relationships dominate. As Hannah Arendt demonstrated in *Eichmann in Jerusalem: A Study in the Banality of Evil* (1964), such ruler-subject relationships may generate patterns of thought and behavior—such as Jewish submissive-

---

[12] Talcott Parsons, *Structure and Process in Modern Societies* (New York, 1960), p. 180.

ness to Nazis, even in the face of death by mass gassing—that facilitate smooth functioning of the state's machinery of control. To similar effect, the record suggests that chattel slavery tended to produce apathy and fecklessness in American blacks.[13] Such a syntax, in which attitudes articulated with society's needs—and helped prevent slave uprisings at the same time—was all to the good so far as the functioning of antebellum Southern society was concerned.

The buyer-seller and ruler-subject concepts can also be used in analyzing changes over time. Since such an analysis is presented in the chapters that follow, it might be helpful to give a simple illustration.

Sir Henry Maine's *Ancient Law* (1861) remains among the most imposing structures on the bridge between archaeology-anthropology and legal history. Maine's dictum, "the movement of the progressive societies has hitherto been a movement from Status to Contract,"[14] asserted a historical shift from dominance of the ruler-subject mode to a situation in which the social syntax develops around the buyer-seller mode. Maine saw ancient society as a dark world of individuals bound into hostile, or at least alien, clans. In each kin group, behavior followed paternal whim:

> So far as regards the person, the parent, when our information commences, has over his children the . . . power of life and death, and *a fortiori* of uncontrolled corporal chastisement; he can modify their personal condition at pleasure; he can give a wife to his son; he can give his daughter in marriage, . . . he can transfer them to another family by adoption; and he can sell them.

Thus "by the behests of a despot enthroned by each hearthstone" were prescribed all rights, duties, and privileges. This was a status-dominated society, with ruler-subject compulsions at every turn, and ruled by the extended family's paterfamilias.

[13] See particularly Stanley M. Elkins, *Slavery* (Chicago, 1959), chap. 3, esp. pp. 133-139.

[14] Henry Maine, *Ancient Law* (London, 1924), p. 174.

According to Maine, the hallmark of "progressive" societies has been substitution of the individual, a free bargaining agent, for the family as the basic legal unit: "We seem to have steadily moved towards a phase of social order in which . . . relations arise from the free agreement of Individuals"[15]—toward a syntax in which institutionalized exchange becomes society's basic means of creating and enforcing rights. The primacy of exchange fell little short of American constitutional orthodoxy under Chief Justice John Marshall, as will be shown in Chapter IV.

Because the transactional mode is fundamental to a given society, one might study Institutions in terms of the transactions in which they specialize. Such Institutions as commodity and stock markets, banks, employment agencies and labor unions, cartels, and merchandising firms facilitate buyer-seller transactions. Armies and navies are Institutions which specialize in the ruler-subject transaction. Other Institutions with relatively "pure" functions are grant-awarding foundations (Carnegie, Rockefeller, Ford) and charitable services (Salvation Army, Community Chest), which clearly lie in the donor-donee category.

But most Institutions have mixed rather than pure functions. Marriage, which is both a foundational institution in every society and, in each actual nuptial union, an Institution in the organic sense, partakes of at least three modes. Family law retains vestiges of the ancient ruler-subject model, in which—though Maine overstated the point—the father enjoyed dominion over all aspects of the household. The notion of the husband as head of the house gives evidence of a residual *patria potesta.*

The view that marriage is also a contractual exchange of rights and duties between husband and wife has grown with the emancipation of women and the decline of earlier Christian ideals, with their lacing of the Pauline doctrine of female subservience. The contract view is dominant in Western societies, where the practice of overtly "arranged" marriages has fallen into desuetude. But weddings made in

[15] *Ibid.,* pp. 145, 171-172.

parents' counting rooms or over two families' chessboards of dynastic interests, or in primitive societies that employ bride-price and similar institutions,[16] also owe much to the buyer-seller model.

But if the exchange of vows between two emancipated partners normally satisfies the two requisites of the buyer-seller relation, mutuality and reciprocity, it is also true that marriage is more than a hardheaded trade. A successful song of the 1967 American popular music season, entitled "Gentle on My Mind," begins with:

> It's knowing that your door is always open and
> 　　your path is free to walk,
> That makes me tend to leave my bag rolled up
> 　　and stashed behind your couch.
> And it's knowing I'm not shackled by forgotten
> 　　words and bonds, and the ink stains
> 　　that are dried upon some line,
> That keeps you in the backroads by the rivers
> 　　of my memory, and keeps you ever
> 　　gentle on my mind.

The song is unequivocally "anti-marriage" in the sense of a formalized, binding, contractual agreement. It celebrates living together as a manifestation of pure giving: without benefit of clergy, we are to suppose, but on that sign too, without bargaining before or strings after the fact.

The "Gentle on My Mind" theme, needless to say, is but symptomatic of underlying forces for social change. More significant than the lyrics' substantive implication is their open flouting of the received forms. We find manifested in their forms both the values and symbols by which a culture lives, and the rules and Institutions by which a society conserves itself. This is why "Gentle on My Mind" is, in the

---

[16] Walter Goldschmidt, in *Sebie Law* (Berkeley, 1967), p. 239, gives a striking example from this East African tribe: "Each man is born of a marriage in which he forms a part of the return on an investment made by the father in the mother. The marriage relationship is validated through the payment of a bride-price for which he is the essential quid pro quo. . . . [H]e has a pecuniary value."

strictest and most meaningful sense, as revolutionary in purport as is any modern folk singer's more explicit call to the barricades. Though ostensibly individualistic in its rejection of society's standards, the song is fundamentally an exercise in social doctrine, for it espouses basic changes in the accepted and shared formulas to be applied to continuing social Institutions.

[3]

All Societies Legislate, Even if Only Informally, a "Law of Rules" Prescribing Behavioral Formulas to Govern Situations Encountered in Day-to-Day Life

Man is a social animal, dependent on his fellows. To be in society is a condition of life, perhaps not the sufficient condition, but surely a necessary one. Let us follow some implications of this need.

Most social transactions do not occur randomly. Society holds together only if each member can make more or less accurate predictions about others' behavior. Behavioral regularity is essential in order to prevent chaos in the relations of men, to say nothing of its crucial bearing on the individual's own sense of adequacy and stability. The importance of the imperative of predictability has been implicit in anthropology from the first, and especially in the functionalist approach.[17]

Indeed, cars *do* drive on the right-hand side of the road (or on the left—but uniformly, as the society decrees). Workers *do* normally come to work on time. Merchants normally *do* stay within general bounds of veracity when advertising their wares. In these, as in most other areas of social life, violation of established behavioral rules invites disaster, reprisals, or punishment.

Ruth Benedict has written of the formidably large "arc of culture," or logically possible ways in which human be-

[17] Emile Durkheim, *The Rules of Sociological Method* (New York, 1895, 1958); Malinowski, *Savage Society* and other works; A. R. Radcliffe-Brown, *A Natural Science of Society* (New York, 1948, 1958), esp. p. 99.

ings might manage their affairs.[18] It is culture's task to organize a pattern of life by selecting from this arc of possibilities an integrated set of behavioral rules. Of the actions performed by any individual in a single day, the percentage of those which he would even consider performing in violation of the culturally prescribed "correct" way is exceedingly small. Indeed, it has been said that a person's "culture" is whatever might have been predicted about his behavior on the day he is born: whether he (she) will wear pants or skirts (skirts or pants); develop a taste for (aversion to) caterpillar larvae; marry one wife (one husband) or more; and so forth.

The imperative of predictability is generally satisfied even when not backed by legal sanctions. People find compliance to be to their advantage. They evolve rules of conduct. In a given culture, these rules can often be taken as characteristic of, because generally deemed appropriate to, whatever mode of social transaction is thought to be dominant in most situations to which the rule applies.

Frequently each mode will have generated a different rule, even when the net effects of allocations (in terms of the values transacted) under the different modes do not vary. For example, a commonly transacted value in all societies, sexual gratification, is allocable under any of the modes: rape (ruler-subject); prostitution (buyer-seller); free tryst (donor-donee); and in some cultures by levirate or sororal access to a sibling's spouse (patron-protégé). In each case, the allocation is the same: male gets something from female. Under some conditions in certain cultures, each mode is a legitimate means of transacting the value in question—the medieval *jus primae noctis* in the West being, in effect, an example of legitimized rape. Yet plainly, different rules normally apply both to the permissibility and the appropriate conduct of the transaction, depending on the mode used. In other words, *rules of behavior are often specifically adapted to the mode of transaction rather than to*

[18] Ruth Benedict, *Patterns of Culture* (New York, 1934, 1959), p. 35.

the kind or amount of good transacted. Such rules, as contradistinguished from rules tailored to, say, the transactors' social statuses or the particular value involved in a given transaction, may be termed "modal rules."

Examples of modal rules are all about. They are part of any society's culture, and often transcend different aspects of a culture. There exists an unspoken but well-understood rule in most societies that individuals in the preliminary stages of a buyer-seller transaction may, perhaps *must*, bargain with each other. Ritualized haggling is a familiar institution, from the bazaars of Baghdad to Los Angeles' unnumbered used-car lots.

Marketplace bargaining is a protection for the buyer, a test of skill for the seller, and often a source of entertainment for both. Yet if one adheres to the bargaining rule in donor-donee or ruler-subject situations, he is covered with opprobrium or penalized by his superior. Courtesy requires the donee not to bargain with a potential donor. The merchant who bargains hard, calculates a competitive profit margin, and drives a good deal, gains a reputation for hardheadedness, agility, and practicality. But the dinner-party guest who sends back his plate, or the recipient of an act of generosity who "looks a gift horse in the teeth," is set down as a lout.

For another example, the rule of *caveat emptor,* "Let the buyer beware," moderates the buyer-seller transaction as a follow-through to bargaining. Haggling favors the buyer; *caveat emptor,* the seller. This rule, reflecting belief in the sound policy of having a clear end-point for any sale, assigns the buyer responsibility for insuring an article's fitness before purchase. Otherwise a vendor, even though not accused of fraud, might be liable indefinitely to make good for alleged defects. Such liability would undercut the tradesman's security of profit and his ability to compute his assets on the basis of past sales preparatory to laying future entrepreneurial plans.

Such a rule, for whatever reason initially formulated, works today because it facilitates the performance of a needed function in a mercantile society. Moreover, this norm, as a legal rule, is further supported by "echoing" rules which moderate apparently disparate behavior (though behavior still in the buyer-seller mode). That such echoes are sometimes discovered in the least likely sectors or strata of society gives evidence of the reach of syntactical pressures. The following excerpt from Iona and Peter Opie's study of the social norms of English youngsters, *The Lore and Language of Schoolchildren*, exemplifies the point: "The chief bargains made at school concern swapping. . . . And the anxiety of those who swap is centered on the knowledge that after a while one party or the other is apt to regret his bargain and want back, indeed demand back, what has been exchanged." Most playground sayings associated with trading are actually ritualized ways of putting the transactors on notice that *caveat emptor*, the functional rule, is also the resolving formula: "Tin tacks, no backs" among children in Peterborough; "Tick tack, never give back, or God will send you down below" in Dublin; and in Croydon:[19]

> Touch teeth, touch leather,
> No backsies for ever and ever.

Any number of more highly formalized rules—usually expressed in some arcane language, whether that of lawyers or of school kids—perform the same function.

But if *caveat emptor* is thought fitting in the exchange situation, a contrary and almost unlimited liability to redress wrongs is borne by government in the Anglo-American tradition. The ruler's, the sovereign's, the government's resources far outweigh those of any individual. Their mistakes are likely to be far more damaging, and their actions, if mean or venal, far more reprehensible. Government does not need the same solicitude as does the flea-market salesman, so the opposite rule to *caveat emptor* applies to ruler-subject transactions between state and citizen.

[19] Iona and Peter Opie, *The Lore and Language of School Children* (Oxford, 1959), p. 132.

Provisions for pardons and reprieves insure that a case can always be reopened in the citizen's favor, just as the constitutional prohibition of double jeopardy helps implement the asymmetrical obverse side of this notion by preventing a case from being reopened in the state's favor. The layman's meaning of "due process of law" is often simply that the government must never take unfair advantage of its superior powers. Justice Holmes' assertion in a 1928 wiretap case dissent that he would rather "some criminals escape than that the Government play an ignoble part"[20] appealed to this sense that government must be upright, and willing, if need be, to bend backwards in the defendant's interest.

The artful sharper may be an accepted and colorful figure in the arcades. But his cunning has no place in government, not in a society whose children start learning the norm of "fair play" from their earliest childhood socialization experiences.

[4]
Underlying Law Are "Rules" Manifesting Society's Need for Behavioral Predictability, Orderly Allocations of Value and Cultural Coherence

At every turn individuals confront informal, unconsciously observed norms of behavior, reminiscent of William Graham Sumner's theme that "folkways" or "mores" really govern society.[21] We may draw from the preceding discussion five propositions that will prove useful throughout the following analysis.

1. *"Culture Lag."* As indicated, a society tends to organize around one predominant mode of social organization. By responding to such imperatives of a viable society as behavioral predictability and orderly allocations of value over time, the society's members develop values, attitudes, and beliefs appropriate to that mode. Although it is in no case

---

[20] *Olmstead* v. *U.S.*, 277 U.S. 438, 470.
[21] William Graham Sumner, *Folkways* (Boston, 1906, 1940), pp. 1-4 and chap. 2.

the exclusive means of allocating values, and is not always even apparent in its pervasiveness, the dominant mode will furnish an integrating matrix for the development of rules, institutions, and Institutions. It also generates a web of characteristic, more or less consistent, attitudes and values among society's members.

But society and culture respond differentially to different influences. History shows many instances of societies' adjusting the actual modes of allocating goods and services to take advantage of an advancing technology, while leaving their laws and rules in the old forms. This calls to mind William F. Ogburn's "cultural lag" concept,[22] which refers to the gap between what society actually is at some point in time and obsolescent beliefs regarding what it is or should be. We shall explore the results of the frequent tendency of the Supreme Court, as the official rule-interpreter and therefore oracle of American political culture, to be not merely a victim but also a cause of such lags.

2. *Functional Integration.* Building on the first proposition, society may be viewed *analytically* as a network of value-transactions among individuals; *formally*, as a "program" for these interactions, like a complicated (and incompletely "debugged") computer program consisting of rules to guide and render predictable the behavior of transacting persons; *behaviorally*, as the regularized activity patterns which evidence the rules' existence, extent, and strength; and *organically*, as a set of Institutions composed of persons performing specific and sometimes specialized functions, much as body organs work together performing separate but complementary functions.

Transactions, rules, institutions, and Institutions tend to articulate with one another. Indeed, they are manifestations of one another as different forms and different aspects of the same society. For this reason alone we would expect them to be integrated into a coherent whole. Such integration does not occur with mechanical precision, as sometimes seemed to be implied by functionalists of the Malinowski

---

[22] William F. Ogburn, *Social Change* (Huebsch, 1922), esp. pt. 4.

and Radcliffe-Brown schools. But integration is often suffi-
ciently pronounced to reflect an underlying harmony of
operation and objective. Culture, so far as it responds to
syntactical pressures that it generates itself, tends to
change in a direction that will increase this harmony. Activities are more or less "functional" as this harmony is more
or less complete.

3 *"Function" and the Group Sense.* Rules—an element
of culture—help insure and regularize performance of certain functions. A. R. Radcliffe-Brown, a seminal theorist of
functionalism, once defined function as "the total set of relations that a single social activity or usage or belief has to the
total social system."[23] In this book, function has a narrower,
though still broad, meaning. It is defined as a given activity's contribution to the allocation of values in a society. In
this definition, the concept of society is as important as are
those of allocation and value. *Functional behavior, therefore, is at minimum behavior resulting in allocations that
tend to perpetuate the members' sense of common identity
with the society.*

This identity or group sense is never complete. Which is
to say that culture is never perfectly coherent. Society is
never fully synchronized. Nor are its rules fully shared, its
institutions uniformly practiced, its members' behavior
completely predictable. But individuals' sense of common
group membership can meaningfully be said to be more or
less profound, given an antecedent definition of the group
itself. Such a shared identity can also be hypothesized as increasing or decreasing in a group, depending on variations
in its allocation of values.

4. *The Link Between Value and Function.* Functional
behavior is usually behavior in accordance with rules. Rules
reflect shared norms. And each individual's conformity to
group behavioral norms tends to strengthen the members'
sense of common identity, if only by dramatizing their existence as a group by acceding to mandates which would not
exist but for the group. What is functional is therefore spe-

[23] A. R. Radcliffe-Brown, *A Natural Science of Society,* p. 85.

cific to the society in question. A certain activity cannot be posited as functional for all societies except in trivial cases, e.g., members of all societies must eat.

In an ideally integrated society, with all behavior machine-like and absolutely predictable, all behavior would be functional. Although no society attains or even approximates such integration, all societies' rules strain toward a working syntax. Thus the Law of Rules embodies both a union and a tension between function and value—as indeed do a society's formal "laws," which are rooted in and reflect the rules.

5. *Modes, Rules, and Mental Sets.* The final proposition approaches the same point by a different path. A modal rule tends to apply to all behavior within the mode, regardless of disparities and differences among values or participants in the transaction. Put differently, the different modes of behavior generate characteristic, repetitive modes of thought, i.e., mental sets. A market is a market, and buyer-seller rules will often be applied formula-fashion, whether the goods traded are Idaho potatoes, Xerox stock certificates, African slaves, or colored beads for Manhattan island. Resolving formulas tend to generalize. Rules cross the boundaries between different sectors and segments of society, as exemplified in the reliance of school children and professional merchants alike on appropriately expressed formalizations of the *caveat emptor* rule. In a word, rules are socially integrative. This is now seen largely to follow from the fact that rules are behaviorally predictive.

We may now begin to build a theory of law that will help interpret American constitutional development. A rule will often, if by no means always, moderate a particular mode of transaction. Using the horizontal dimension of the following diagram to show the effect of transactions on the state of the system (allocations of values), and the vertical dimension to show their cumulative effect on the system's operation (evolved rules to guide behavior in future transactions), the twofold impact of transactions can be depicted:

Transactions → Allocations
     |
Rules - - - - - - -↑

"Law" serves a mediating function in this system. It aims to channel behavior in the most socially significant transactions into regularized, and if need be enforced, compliance with the rules.

Law seeks to insure that society's allocations occur in accordance with the rules, as in the dashed path of the diagram, rather than, as in the solid arrow, immediately from unregulated transactions. The fact that law performs this function, rather than any particular normative content in the rules that it implements, establishes it in a given society as "authoritative." The means employed in the U.S. constitutional system to enable law to accomplish this function supply the subject of the pages that follow.

[CHAPTER III]

THE FRAMERS'
POLITICAL SYNTAX

THE AIM of this chapter is to reconstruct the framers' achievement in combining received doctrines and attitudes into the Constitution of 1787, which both reflected the early Americans' political culture and served their national aspirations. This early resonance between culture and constitution is summarized in the notion of the framers' "political syntax." (Henceforth "Constitution" will be capitalized only when referring to the framers' document; "constitution," uncapitalized, will refer to the entire body of authoritative interpretations of the limits of public power— including, but not limited to, those of the Supreme Court and those explicitly imported by the words of the Constitution itself.)

[1]
The Norm of Limited Government, an Anti-statist Attitude, and the Belief that Government is Inherently Negative Dominated the Framers' Political Culture

As laws are rooted in and reflect the rules, a working constitution must reflect its ambient culture—if, that is, it is to continue to work. As indicated in Chapter II, the term culture in this book refers to learned norms, attitudes, and beliefs shared by the individuals in a given society. "Political culture" refers to learned norms, attitudes, and beliefs about how power should and should not be used. Thus political culture influences the form and frequency, the permissibility of and participation in, the transactions whereby values are allocated.

"If men were angels, there would be no need for government," Madison wrote in *Federalist* No. 51. But men's tendency to give evil for good, or at least to exceed their rightful powers, required government to mediate relations between man and man. Madison's pessimism about human nature had creditable pedigrees in received philosophy. Hobbes characterized life in the state of nature as "nasty, . . . brutish and short."[1] The more temperate Locke thought the nongovernmental state at best "inconvenient" and insecure.[2] Even the normally optimistic Jefferson shared most early Americans' assumption that men, left to their own devices, tended to mutual destructiveness. "The tree of liberty," Jefferson asserted, "must be refreshed from time to time with the blood of tyrants and patriots."[3] It followed that "free government is founded in jealousy, and not in confidence; it is jealousy and not confidence which prescribes limited constitutions, to bind down those whom we are obliged to trust with power: . . . In questions of power, then, let no more be heard of confidence in man, but bind him down from mischief by the chains of the Constitution."[4] Jefferson's distrust of power, his anti-statism, summed up a characteristic American response and furnished a unifying principle of the framers' political syntax. Embodied in the structure of checks and balances, anti-statism offered a clear and, in the circumstances of early America, a functionally satisfactory answer to the problem of reconciling "the public good and private rights."[5] Moreover, anti-statism emerged as a lowest common denominator from the main competing approaches to political theory current in the framers' day.

How were they to reconcile order with liberty? How to interweave ruler-subject restraints into society's network of free buyer-seller relationships? Two lines of approach suggested themselves. One viewed the state as a device to achieve utilitarian goals; the other, associated with the Puritan tradition, saw the state as an agent of Divine Will or a moral instrument.

Eighteenth-century Utilitarians, following Adam Smith and Jeremy Bentham, tended to view the state as a party in

[1] *Leviathan*, pt. I, chap. 13.
[2] *Second Treatise on Civil Government*, chap. 2, sec. 13.
[3] To William Stephens Smith, November 13, 1787. 12 Boyd 356.
[4] Kentucky Resolution (1798). *Writings* 7 (Ford ed.), 288, 309.
[5] See Madison in *Federalist* No. 10.

a buyer-seller transaction. Government was like a big joint stock company, similar to A.T. & T. or General Motors, but producing law and order instead of telephone service or automobiles. Government could probably never be so efficient, by this view, as a well-managed industrial firm—a belief that by no means passed with the eighteenth century. Nevertheless Adam Smith in *Wealth of Nations* (1776) admitted that the state alone could provide certain necessary services (italicized below):[6]

> According to the system of natural liberty, the sovereign has only three duties to attend to; . . . first, the duty of *protecting the society* from violence and invasion of other independent societies; secondly, the duty of protecting, as far as possible, every member of society from the injustice or oppression of every other member of it, or the duty of establishing an exact *administration of justice;* and, thirdly, the duty of *erecting and maintaining certain public works* and certain public institutions, which it could never be for the interest of any individual, or small number of individuals, to erect and maintain; because the profit could never repay the expense to any individual or small number of individuals, though it may frequently do much more than repay it to a great society.

Most activities in Smith's categories are "natural monopolies," requiring investment on so large a scale as to prevent individual ownership or competition among several private firms.

Moreover the benefits of common defense and administration of justice are commonly shared. Every loyal citizen gains a sense of security if the army deters enemy attack. Everyone (ironically, even criminals) shares in the advantages of domestic law and order.[7] These benefits are indivisible. Individuals cannot buy them in increments, the way

[6] *Wealth of Nations*, bk. IV, chap. 9.

[7] See Mancur Olson, *The Logic of Collective Action* (Cambridge, Mass., 1964) for the best and most original systematic exposition of "the theory of public goods."

a housewife buys coffee or flour. Instead the citizenry (or electorate) as a whole must make a collective purchase by pooling resources (a bit from each through taxes), and through the central instrumentality of the state produce or procure the needed public services. Under Utilitarian theory, government action is advocated on grounds not of desirability (except in a nonethical sense of "efficiency"), but of necessity.

Classical economic theory, the intellectual matrix of laissez-faire, biased political doctrines proceeding from it against public power except on a showing that equivalent service could not be provided as efficiently by private (entrepreneurial) initiative. Early American subscribers to this theory wanted to yield the central government only such powers as were clearly necessary and could not in their nature be assumed at state or local levels, lest public power be expanded beyond real need. From this Utilitarian approach, indeed, we get the idea of federalism.

Proceeding from an opposite starting point, but reaching a conclusion similar in some respects to the Utilitarian theory, is a view of the state as the civil instrument of "essential justice." Righteousness, not efficiency, is thus the end of the state, which itself is a moral entity, not merely a political artifice designed to do jobs that could not be done as well (or at all) by private persons or lesser governmental units.[8]

In the extreme form, as under the Puritans, the state is regarded as a set of sanctions waiting to happen to transgressors. The Cambridge Platform of 1648 asserted: "Idolatry, Blasphemy, Heresy, venting corrupt & pernicious opinions, . . . prophanation of the Lord's day, disturbing the peaceable administration of the worship & holy things of God, the like, are to be restrayned & punished by civil authority."[9] Deriving from the same doctrinal predilections, the Puri-

[8] Perry Miller, *Errand Into the Wilderness* (New York, 1956, 1964), p. 143.

[9] Quoted in George Athan Bliss, ed., *Law and Authority in Colonial America* (Barre, Mass., 1965), p. 141.

tans made an enduring contribution to the rules governing bargaining and exchange. Roscoe Pound observed that Puritanism:[10]

> has given us the notion of punishing the vicious will and the necessary connection between wrong doing and retribution. . . . The Puritan has always been a consistent and thoroughgoing opponent of equity. It runs counter to all his ideas. For one thing, it helps fools who have made bad bargains, whereas he believes that fools should be allowed and required to act freely and then be held for the consequences of their folly.

Caveat emptor is a rule of law, an echo of history, a reflection of culture—all three.

Both Utilitarianism and Puritanism attempted, each after its fashion, to maximize individual freedom and happiness. Puritanism looked to a stern sort of freedom and happiness: freedom for each to live in earnest godliness, being damned well happy doing it or most likely being damned anyway. Extreme economic individualism, following laissez-faire Utilitarianism, in time led to even grimmer results than did Puritanism, and was memorialized in Anatole France's perhaps apocryphal comment to the effect that freedom in nineteenth-century "liberal" systems amounted to the equal liberty of rich and poor alike to sleep under bridges.

Moreover, both approaches assumed as an achievable condition, if not ever as an accomplished fact, a social harmony or equilibrium toward which a well-ordered society tended. Adam Smith's disciples had resolute faith in the Invisible Hand. Provided each individual was equally resolute in pursuing his own self-interest, the Invisible Hand would harmonize the social apparatus into a smoothly functioning economy.[11] The equilibrium thus achieved would, with minimum public interference, yield greatest happiness

---

[10] Roscoe Pound, *The Spirit of the Common Law* (Boston, 1921), pp. 44-45, 53.

[11] *Wealth of Nations*, bk. IV, chap. 2.

to the greatest number. Less obviously but just as surely, Puritan theory implied limited government too. John Cotton, clerical mouthpiece of early Massachusetts' theocracy, preached "that all power that be on earth be limited." Thomas Hooker's tract, *Limitation of Government*, foreshadowed the American doctrine of public power constrained as well as energized by fundamental principles of right.[12]

Exponents of natural law, like believers in divine law, thought justice to lie in harmony between society's actual working and some ethical standard. To achieve such harmony, government might have to assume substantial and tutelary responsibilities, as in Puritan theory. Natural law theorists like Locke and Jefferson envisaged a smaller role for public power. But whatever the needed scope of public action, once government reached that limit its duties ended. Thus the ideal of limited government emerged by implication from both approaches, which combined to generate an attitude of hostility and suspicion, negativism and antistatism. This attitude that the state is inherently repressive or inevitably inefficient had no less important a part than did the norm of limited government in rendering thematically coherent America's early political culture.

In addition to norms and attitudes, culture includes those beliefs about what actually "is" which are generally shared by the members of a society. The framers were not utopians. They did not believe in human generosity and self-lessness as valid bases for society. They therefore placed no reliance on the donor-donee relationship as a model for governmental structure. Nor does the patron-protégé mode figure prominently, except in a special interpretation of this concept to be advanced in Chapter VI. But the buyer-seller and ruler-subject models offered fruitful suggestions for constitutional engineering.

The buyer-seller category corresponded to two principal elements of the American system—the contract basis of gov-

12 Cotton and Hooker quotations are from A. T. Mason, *Free Government in the Making* (New York, 1965), pp. 53-54.

ernment and the service orientation of many government activities. The ruler-subject category accommodated, first, the principle of popular sovereignty which subordinates government to the people; and second, the principle of "rule of law" which subordinates all individuals to duly enacted rules of behavior promulgated by the government. Government activity under the latter heading may be further partitioned into prospective rule-making, which is a legislative function, and retrospective rule-interpretation, which is judicial in nature. This division corresponds to a distinction at the heart of the concept of separation of powers. The remainder of this chapter develops these distinctions in a model of the American political system which highlights three dualities: buyer-seller versus ruler-subject relationships; "services" versus "sanctions"; and judicial versus political checks on government.

[2]

The "Political" Check on Government, Exerted at the Ballot Box, Uses the Buyer-Seller Pattern by Relying on the Theory of Contract and the Institutions of Bargaining

"We, the People" are the source of all powers delegated to the arms of government, with substantive and initiative responsibilities. These are the legislative, which makes laws; and the executive, which oversees faithful execution of the laws and exercises substantive powers in the conduct of foreign affairs and as commander-in-chief of the army, navy, and air force.

The official activities of these branches fall into two categories. First, there are those acts whose dominant effects are to regulate, restrain, or control. Henceforth, such acts will be termed *sanctions*, with a negative valence, in that they require or prohibit certain actions under threat of penalty or retaliation. Examples include the Prohibition Acts of the 1920's and prohibitions of racially discriminatory behavior under civil rights laws. Second, government provides certain *services*, such as support for education and technology under the Morrill Act of 1862, establishing "land grant colleges"; acquisition and dissemination of useful knowledge (the Smithsonian Institution; Federal scholarship funds under the National Defense Education Act); agricultural extension services; postal and maritime subsidies; and perhaps most important of all, social security and unemployment programs.

Should the legislature or executive take an action that presumes powers clearly beyond those granted in the Constitution, so long as the issue can be raised as a case suitable for judicial determination,[13] a court exercising the power of judicial review can declare the act void. This is the *judicial* check. On the other hand, if the legislature or executive, operating within its constitutionally allowable sphere, acts contrary to popular will, the people can throw the government out of office at the next election. This is the *political* check, which is primary in the American system.

The political check presumes a "contract" whereby people agree to delegate certain powers in exchange for useful services from the governors, such as maintenance of domestic order and protection from foreign invasion. The political contract has generated modes of behavior associated with the buyer-seller transaction. For example, in the formation of a government there is implicit bargaining between potential rulers (who make campaign promises) and those to be ruled (who vote for candidates offering what appears to be the preferable program). The rulers' tenure in office partly depends on how well they deliver on their side of the bargain.

U.S. electoral Institutions point up the central roles of bargaining, contracting, even "candidate marketing" in the government-forming process. Prominent American extra-constitutional Institutions are parties and pressure groups. The goal of parties is the acquisition of power. But their main functions include recruiting potential governors and then attempting to sell them to the electorate. Political

[13] See the discussion in *Baker* v. *Carr*, 369 U.S. 186, 198-204 (1962), and Brandeis in *Ashwander* v. *T.V.A.*, 297 U.S. 288, 345-348 (1936).

parties thus develop "products" (namely, candidates and programs) for which a demand is thought to exist; they advertise to convince voters that their products are superior; and they try to insure adequate quality once the product is bought (for example, by trying to enforce party discipline so that programs will pass in the legislature), lest voters or "customers" switch brands at the next election. Just as a firm is punished with declining profits if it does not better the competition's product, so is the "in" party punished with defeat if its standard-bearers do not deliver on pre-election promises.

Parties essentially perform marketing or exchange rather than governing functions. It is therefore not by coincidence that political science literature on parties frequently draws on economics for explanatory hypotheses and couches its findings in the vocabulary of economics.[14] Substantial areas of U.S. constitutional law can be explained as formal—and sometimes inappropriate—applications of norms developed for the buyer-seller transaction to a political process, election.

To sum up, then: the basic reliance of American political theory for limitation of government is placed on the concept of consent, a concept owing far more to the buyer-seller than to the ruler-subject model. To the extent that the notion of consent and hence of a political check on government, has been relied on, the Utilitarian approach has prospered. This has been at the expense of the Puritan bias toward ideas of "truth" and "justice" independent of popular will. The latter bias has always buttressed the judicial check as a guarantor of essential justice against majority deprivation.

But both Utilitarian and Puritan approaches inclined American politics away from the "service" orientation, preferring such activities to be performed by private enterprise, or not at all. There began to emerge, then, two antin-

[14] E.g., Anthony Downs, *An Economic Theory of Democracy* (New York, 1957); Gerald Garvey, "Theory of Party Equilibrium," *Amer. Pol. Sci. Rev.* 60 (March 1966), 29, and sources cited there.

omies, anchored in the modes of social transaction discussed in Chapter II and in the political culture that straddled the Utilitarian and Puritan approaches to government. These antinomies—political check versus judicial check, and services versus sanctions as the dominant preoccupation of American government—underlie some basic, often bitter, disputes of American constitutional history. We now turn to the poles of these antinomies which derive from the ruler-subject model.

[3]

As Public Law Presupposes a Legitimized Ruler-Subject Relationship, its History May Be Analyzed as a Pattern of Changes in the Concepts Governing the Nature and Uses of Public Power

Limited government can be maintained by power as well as by contract. Indeed, it implies a continuing and inviolable ruler-subject hierarchy. The people in their corporate political capacity serve as a collective "ruler," with government subject to their will as embodied in the Constitution. At the same time, government exercises power over individuals qua individuals.

Power suggests the ruler's ability to restrict the subject's freedom. Technically, power presupposes that some actor (the ruler) wholly or partly determines which alternatives the subject must evaluate prior to choosing his course of action. This formulation describes an essential element in the phenomenon of power as the word is normally understood, yet preserves free will for the actors. Thus, to be a ruler is to possess the ability to force another to consider options that he would not otherwise consider. In most cases the forced option has negative value for the subject (like getting fined if he takes some action the ruler forbids, or being clubbed on the head, or going to jail). Because bluffing by a ruler is usually eventually found out, a ruler normally also has the ability actually to impose the threatened sanctions if the subject does not comply.

It results that each individual confronts at all times a set of possible actions which may be exhaustively divided into the subset of all actions with which he associates positive value, and the complementary subset of all possible options to which he assigns negative value. Ruler-subject transactions include any in which sanctions are effectively threatened or actually imposed, contingent on some subject's pursuing or not pursuing a course of action pro- or prescribed by the ruler. As indicated in Chapter II, in some cases power also implies transactions in which a subject is induced to take or rewarded for having taken options that have negative valence for him. Table II shows the resulting categories.[15]

(a) *Deterrence and Retaliation.* First are situations in which the ruler threatens or imposes sanctions to prevent or punish a subject for behaving in a manner not desired by the ruler but desired by the subject. Applied prospectively, as a threat, this is deterrence. Actual imposition of the sanction after the subject has committed a prohibited act is retaliation.

Table II. *Six Categories of Power*

| Valence to Subject of: | | Time Frame of Exercise of Power | |
Value Offered or Imposed	Action Required or Performed	Prospective	Retrospective
−	+	Deterrence	Retaliation
−	−	Coercion	Penalty
+	−	Bribery	Reward

As a legal concept, retaliation is preserved in the ancient *lex talionis*—the law of retribution often found at the basis of primitive legal systems,[16] and fundamental to Biblical

[15] For a more complete treatment, including development of the mathematical formulation of the power concept, see Gerald Garvey, "Domain of Politics," *Western Political Quarterly* (March 1970).

[16] Alfred Radcliffe-Brown suggested this as a possible basis for a unifying theory of society; see *A Natural Science of Society* (New York, 1948, 1957), pp. 132ff.

justice ("An eye for an eye," Exod. 21:23). Retaliatory law has an obvious bearing on Anglo-American criminal justice, highlighted in modern controversies over capital punishment; and it even influences civil law, as in allowances for punitive damage awards in libel or slander cases.

The deterrent and retaliatory categories derive much of their strength in American jurisprudence from the early, especially the Puritan, conviction of human depravity. Behind legal systems animated primarily by deterrence and retaliation—and the same may be said of broader political systems, such as the "balance of terror" system of international nuclear politics—is a belief that men are basically aggressive, that if unrestrained by combined threats and experiences of punishment their actions will be inimical to the rights of others.

(b) *Coercion and Penalty.* In the next category, sanctions are threatened to get a subject to perform some act which he would otherwise prefer not to do. This is coercion or, when applied retrospectively, penalty. While deterrent and retaliatory systems may be supported by little beyond a sense of fear—as in Hobbes, for example—coercion and penalty as here defined presume at least a rudimentary sense of society and of its positive needs. The presupposition is that performing certain acts is as necessary as refraining from anti-social forms of activity. To neglect required behavior is, by this view, as harmful as indulgence in proscribed behavior.

This view of society represents in an obvious sense an advance over the primitive *lex talionis.* And without broaching a "progress theory" of history, it may be pointed out that coercion and penalty become proportionately more important as a society and its legal system grow in complexity and modernity. These categories, for example, embrace most statutes enacted to regulate trade or commerce, most licensing and registration ordinances, and the bulk of "police power" legislation passed by state legislatures from the period of Jacksonian democracy onward (see Chapter v).

(c) *"Bribery" and Reward.* Finally, power situations

often include those in which positive values are promised to induce, or given to repay, a subject for pursuing some action which would otherwise be undesired by him. Prospectively, this is bribery; retrospectively, reward.

Bribery and reward assume an ability, and in some cases a right, in the public authority to extend conditional services. Clearly, the government which provides price supports for farmers exerts power over the agricultural sector. The government that finances research and scholarship enjoys political leverage in the academic community. The government that gives welfare checks to indigents exerts control over life in the nation's slums. How much power to extend such conditional services is appropriate? How is it to be disciplined?

The relevance of these questions evidences that yet another step in the development of American political and constitutional theory has occurred. For they are provoked by the shift in emphasis associated with the New Deal: from *sanctions* (a legal system dominated by the first four categories) to *services* (in which public largesse, because viewed in the post–New Deal era as exactly that, opens new fields for the exercise—and abuse—of power). This development and these questions are treated in Chapter vii.

Thus early American thought was marked by a negativism, a component of both Utilitarian and Puritan thought, which held power to be inherently inefficient or repressive, and wielders of public power to be unenlightened and devoted by their very calling to restraint of human behavior rather than to liberation of the individual's potential. The state was concerned with sanctions, restrictive in tendency and painful in application.

What distinguished Utilitarianism from Puritanism in practice was the larger scope for public action envisioned by the latter. This disposition resulted from the Puritans' less generous view of human nature, corresponding to the difference between downright depravity and enlightened selfishness, and necessitating therefore more controls on behavior. But they shared an aversion to government wherever it was not clearly needed. This goes far to explain both the early bias of American public law and its integration into a syntax patterned on free and individualistic buyer-seller values rather than on the potentially repressive ruler-subject model. The development of this bias during Marshall's chief justiceship is the subject of Chapter IV.

APPENDIX TO CHAPTER III

SEPARATION OF POWERS, FEDERALISM, AND THE DIMENSIONS OF POWER

SEPARATION of powers emerged from the political culture in which the Framers were immersed—and from the literature of Montesquieu and Locke—as a tenet of political morality, and one that embodied a basic norm of "fair play." As expounded by the courts in the early national period, separation of powers implemented a rule of fairness evolved in response to the problem, universal in all societies, of regulating ruler-subject relationships: fair warning must precede punishment, whether retaliation or penalty. A ruler's decrees must therefore be future-oriented. Laws must be promulgated, at least constructively, before they may be enforced, lest any subject be liable to punishment for violating a rule not known and in force at the time of the culpable behavior.

Sir Edward Coke, called the "greatest of the common lawyers," enunciated the principle: "A legislative enactment ought to be prospective, not retrospective in its operation."[17] Joseph Story—with John Marshall, James Kent, and Lemuel Shaw the leader of pre–Civil War America's legal profession—developed the fair-warning rule as a principle of constitutional obligation. Any statute, wrote Story,

[17] 2 *Institutes* 292.

"which takes away or impairs vested rights acquired under existing laws, or creates new obligations, imposes a new duty, or attaches a new disability in respect to transactions or considerations already past, must be deemed retrospective," and for that reason, void.[18]

Supreme Court utterances similar in effect may be found in *Calder* v. *Bull* (1796), in which the Constitution's *ex post facto* clause was first construed,[19] and in *Ogden* v. *Blackledge* (1804). In *Ogden* the Court interrupted counsel who was urging that the division of powers must be maintained and that legislative pronouncements must be prospective. The point, explained the Court, was so obvious as to need no argument.[20] In 1811, the prospective operation requirement became part of New York State's constitutional law through Chancellor Kent's opinion in *Dash* v. *Van Kleeck*.[21] Kent brought not only his prestige as a commentator and judge to the doctrine's support, but also the whole weight of the Western tradition, tracing the rule to the maxim "that the law giver cannot change his mind to the prejudice of a vested right" from Emperor Justinian's *Digest* of Roman Law, published 533 A.D. (Secs. 17, 50, 75).

The prospective requirement not only furnished the source of the Constitution's prohibition of *ex post facto* laws. Far more importantly, as Edward S. Corwin showed, it underlay the so-called "basic doctrine of American constitutional law" as the bulwark of property rights against legislative interference.[22] The main purport of this, the doctrine of vested rights, was that any legislation "unreasonably" trespassing on existing property rights was held to be in effect retrospective, and therefore unconstitutional. "In deed," Corwin asserted, "it is no exaggeration to say that the expulsion of State legislative power from the judicial

[18] *Society* v. *Wheeler*, 2 Gall. (U.S.C.C.) 105, 139 (1814).
[19] See esp. Justice Chase's opinion, 3 Dall. 386, 388-389.
[20] 2 Cr. 272.
[21] 7 Johns (N. Y.) 477.
[22] See Edward S. Corwin, "The Basic Doctrine . . . ," *Michigan Law Review*, 12 (February 1914), 247.

field [via the prospective-retrospective distinction] was the most important by-product of the effort of the State courts between 1800 and the Civil War to provide protection for property rights against that same power."[23]

The rule served to restrain lawmakers by restricting the forms that positive legislation might take. But judges did not "legislate." They were legatees of the medieval notion that human governors had no authority to make laws. They could only discover and declare justice in natural or divine law.[24] James Otis put this point in *Rights of the British Colonies Asserted and Proved* (1764): "The supreme power in a state is *jus dicere* only—*jus dare*, strictly speaking, belongs only to God."[25] From the same tradition of judges as mere mouthpieces of the law came John Marshall's assertion in *Osborne* v. *Bank* (1824): "Judicial power as contradistinguished from the power of the laws, has no existence."[26]

This notion by natural extension gave forth a corollary, that of the courts' exclusive right to express standing law. The result was that an analytical distinction—legislatures act prospectively; courts, only retrospectively—became a rule of law, a normative test of conduct, and one fated to play a prominent role in the history of American constitutional limitations. *Separation of powers, in its distinction between legislative and judicial functions, was but the Institutional embodiment of the analytical distinction between prospective and retrospective exercises of power* as depicted in Table II.

Unlike separation of powers, federalism was a utilitarian invention, justified by Madison in *Federalist* No. 10 as the most practical way to expand the geographic scope of the

[23] *Liberty Against Government* (Baton Rouge, La., 1948), p. 73n. See pp. 61ff. for complete documentation of the sources and early use of the "prospective requirement."

[24] See generally C. H. McIlwain, *The High Court of Parliament and Its Supremacy* (New Haven, 1910), pp. 42-100, passim.

[25] In A. C. McLaughlin, *The Courts, the Constitution, and Parties* (Chicago, 1912), p. 70.

[26] 9 Wheat. 738, 865.

new American nation, so as to "make it less probable that a majority of the whole will have a common motive to invade the rights of other citizens." The "Father of the Constitution's" search for an acceptable federal formula was the search for a workable compromise, not for a principle of justice: "Let it be tried," Madison urged Edmund Randolph before the Philadelphia Convention, "whether any middle ground can be taken, which will at once support a due supremacy of the national authority, and leave in force the local authorities so far as they can be subordinately useful."[27]

But if flexibility was the framers' achievement, vagueness was the price they paid. The "federal contrivance" posed hard questions concerning the distribution of power between nation and states, questions not answered by the words of the Constitution. The national government could use only those powers granted in the Constitution, or reasonably to be inferred therefrom, or "necessary and proper" to carry its granted powers into execution. This left the state legislatures all remaining powers, save as qualified by the respective state constitutions. Because of the "prospective-retrospective" distinction, however, the national legislature's powers might in effect be further circumscribed to the three prospective categories: deterrence, coercion, bribery.

The legislature fell under the further limitations of the Bill of Rights. It could not, for example, deter crime by threatening "cruel or unusual punishments." Congress might exercise its coercive authorities—the majority of its substantive powers by Article I, Section 8 are in the "sanction" rather than the service or buyer-seller categories—only in a manner consistent with all other provisions of the Constitution; it could coerce people into paying taxes, provided that any "capitation or other direct Taxes" were laid "in Proportion to the Census. . . ."

[27] April 8, 1787, *Writings* 2 (Hunt ed.), 336-340.

Finally, American constitutional jurisprudence long reflected the theory, derived from a notion of power as necessarily negative, prohibitory, and constraining, that the nation had no authority to exercise the forms of power defined as "bribery" and "reward." This subject is covered in Chapter VII.

CHAPTER IV

THE LEGAL HUMOUR
IN AMERICA

ALPHEUS T. MASON has written, "Symbolism pervades the judiciary and contributes to its practical effectiveness."[1] To similar effect are the words of Chief Justice William Howard Taft: "It is well that judges should be clothed in robes, . . . in order to impress the judge himself with constant consciousness that he is a high priest in the temple of justice and is surrounded with obligations of a sacred character. . . ."[2] Such attitudes manifest a tendency toward legalism that might have been foreseen from the first. Almost half the signers of the Declaration of Independence were lawyers. More than half of the members of the Constitutional Convention had been trained in law.[3] Legalism in America recalls Dr. Johnson's introduction to *Everyman Out of His Humour*:

> As when some one peculiar quality
> Doth so process a man that it doth draw
> All his affects, his spirits, and his powers,
> In their confluxions, *all to run one way*,
> *This may be truly said to be a humour.*

This chapter considers the "legal humour" in the United States, loosely defined as the inclination of American political energies "all to run one way"—that way being to convert issues of expediency or "functionality" into questions of right, to be resolved not in the political arena but through the judicial process.

[1] Alpheus T. Mason, *The Supreme Court from Taft to Warren* (Baton Rouge, La.: 1958), p. 45.

[2] William H. Taft, *Present Day Problems: A Collection of Addresses.* . . . (New York, 1908), pp. 63-64.

[3] Anton-Hermann Chroust, *The Rise of the Legal Profession in America* (Norman, Okla., 1965), 2: 4-5.

[1]

Rules whose Observance is Especially Important for Society's Smooth Functioning Gain Coercive Backing from the State, Justified as "Right" and Called "Law"

Law grows out of the rules developed to guide behavior into predictable, socially acceptable paths. This does not mean that law merely formalizes custom.[4] It rather means that legal action must not without compelling reason be too widely inconsistent with the society's Law of Rules. This is the point of the familiar assertion that the way to get rid of "bad" laws is not to declare them void, but conscientiously to enforce them and thereby get them repealed. Indeed, this requirement of consistency between Rule of Law and the Law of Rules seems but a broader theoretical statement of the venerable "reasonableness test," taken as a basic judicial standard of a law's validity since Sir Edward Coke celebrated the "artificial reason of the law" in the early seventeenth century.[5]

Rules are enforced through a variety of sanctions: public opinion, magic and sorcery, vengeance against a transgressor, the compulsion of conscience. The Law of Rules does not necessarily have formal, official backing by society's coercive apparatus, usually a government, as does "law" in the sense in which the term will be used in the following discussion. Hence in some stateless societies such as those of the Andaman islanders in the Bay of Bengal or the Sudanese Nuer tribesmen (to use examples familiar in ethnographic literature, thanks to A. R. Radcliffe-Brown and E. E. Evans-Pritchard), there exists no "law." There exists only what Evans-Pritchard called "ordered anarchy,"[6] with

---

[4] See Jerome Frank's critique of the so-called "anthropological theory," and especially of Karl Llewellyn, in *Courts on Trial* (Princeton, 1950), chap. 25. Similar criticism has been leveled—with reason —against W. G. Sumner's theory in *Folkways* (1906).

[5] See Edward S. Corwin, *Liberty Against Government* (Baton Rouge, La., 1948), chap. 1 and pp. 147-148.

[6] A. R. Radcliffe-Brown, *The Andaman Islanders* (Cambridge, 1922), p. 48, and E. E. Evans-Pritchard, *The Nuer* (Oxford, 1940, 1960), p. 6 and chap. 4.

the order coming from widespread observance of general, if uncodified and unrationalized, rules.

Absence of a central coercive authority to insure compliance with rules does not, then, mean that norms exert any less compelling an influence on behavior. Most societies' archives—and certainly America's—are filled with old laws which, though backed by government, proved incapable of attracting respect or commanding obedience. The pre-Civil War fugitive slave laws in some Northern states and the Prohibition era's notoriously unsuccessful Volstead Act readily occur.

Conversely, certain non-legally-enforceable elements of American political culture, because they enjoy a wide supporting consensus, exert a pervasive influence. "Nontoleration of cheaters" or "tattle tale" clauses have brought down honor systems in some colleges and seriously qualified their successes in others, probably because the injunction against tale-bearing is so successfully and deeply internalized in American youth.[7] Miscegenation, though not legally prohibited,[8] remains effectively forbidden over wide areas both in and outside of the South. Examples could be multiplied. Religious as opposed to "legal" rules often furnish bases for accurate predictions about behavior. So do requirements of "class" (*noblesse oblige*; "never sell-out a fellow worker"), and of social status.

Thus the Law of Rules and Rule of Law are neither coextensive in application, nor of equal impact on behavior when they do commonly apply. Nevertheless there exists a mechanism that tends to increase the congruence between customary norms and law in the formal sense. Oliver

[7] A most interesting reflection in this area appears in section VII, "The Cadet Honor Code," in *Report to the Secretary . . . of the Air Force by the Special Advisory Committee on the U.S. Air Force Academy*, May 5, 1965, an analysis of that school's 1965 cheating scandal. Refusal of many cadets to report cheating by their classmates was a main cause of the spread of infractions among the students; and the same dynamic occurred again, though on a smaller scale, in a second cheating scandal of the Academy in February 1967. See *New York Times*, February 25-28, March 2-3, 18.

[8] *Loving* v. *Virginia*, 388 U.S. 112.

Wendell Holmes perhaps had this mechanism in mind when, in 1905, he observed that every opinion tends to become a law.[9] Opinions regarding what is right, expedient, or "fitting" influence behavior. If consistent over time, they generate consistent patterns of behavior. As discussed in Chapter II, such patterns, when observed as characteristic of an individual or group, create expectancies in others. On such expectancies these "others" base their behavior, so that each individual's welfare depends at least in part on the reliability of the resulting patterns of mutual predictability.

Self-interest, custom, and conscience often quite satisfactorily insure the integrity of society's network of mutual reliances. But it is both unwise and unnecessary to rely on chance—or self-interest, custom, or conscience—to insure adherence to rules found to be of particular social significance (e.g., relating to killing or property ownership). Law in the strict sense is needed. The Law of Rules gives way to Rule of Law when a public authority is constituted (or recognized as already existing) and can direct coercive sanctions against individuals who fail to comply with such rules. And thus, although the values served by law must be consistent with those embodied in the society's mores, it is the way that a given value, if acted on or violated, actually functions, rather than the intensity with which it is held as a social consensus, that determines whether or not the rule in question will be selected out to be law.

It is time now to see if this discussion illuminates the functions and gives some perspective to the early achievements of American public law.

[2]

Legalism Responded to the Problem of Insuring the Security of Inequality of Achievement in a Society Philosophically Pledged to Equality of Opportunity

A dominant theme of American constitutional history until 1937—protection of individual property-rights against the democratic masses—was anticipated in the mid-seven-

[9] *Lochner* v. *N. Y.*, 198 U.S. 45, 76 (dissenting).

teenth-century conflict between the "rabble" of Oliver Cromwell's New Model Army and the conservative leadership under Cromwell. The issues joined in mid-seventeenth-century England foreshadowed two ideas: first, the equality of all men ("I think that the poorest he that is in England has a life to live as the richest, he," Thomas Rainboro, a radical debater, argued);[10] and second, the rule of law. The relationship between these ideas is crucial to our story.

Equal standing for all disputants, regardless of disparities in their power or place in society, is a hallmark of law. "Equal Justice Under Law" appears across the lintel of the Supreme Court building in Washington. And equality was the touchstone of radical political philosophy, just as "rule of law" was the radicals' central demand—and for that reason. "Here is their Anarchical Levelling," John Lilburne explained, "that they will endure tyranny, oppression and injustice no more in apostatised Cromwell and Ireton . . . but desire that all alike may be level to and bound by the law."[11] This linking of law with equality is retained to this day in the Anglo-American tradition—with what qualifications and results, we shall consider shortly.

Preoccupation with arbitrary power, if not Lilburne's free-swinging style, anticipated a main theme in American colonial politics. Because of distance from England, administration of justice became an undertaking of the colonists themselves. Americans established their own tradition of rough and ready law. Particularly important were developing legal formulations of rules that supported the old Leveller value of equality in administration of justice, *yet helped maintain orderly patterns of inequality, both of authority and of possession*, essential to the functioning of early American—or for that matter, of any other—society. Fac-

[10] Quoted in A. T. Mason, *Free Government in the Making* (New York, 1964), p. 13.

[11] Quoted in Robertson, *The Religious Foundations of Leveller Democracy* (New York, 1951), pp. 2-3. The best summary of the Leveller-Digger agitation is in Mason, *Free Government in the Making*, chap. 1 through p. 21.

tors inherent in the context of the frontier dictated a reluctance fully to realize the egalitarian potential of a world that was politically "new."

Early America came as close as perhaps any society that the colonists might have imagined to Hobbes' "state of nature." The frontier imperatives were ruggedness and struggle. Life was hard. Often it was violent, dangerous, and hostile. This was the case not least because the colonists achieved something close to an equality of condition, as opposed to an equality of ability. If men were unequal in their abilities to achieve, they were much more nearly equal in their abilities to harm one another—especially on the frontier, where most individuals perforce had both the skills and the weapons of the stalker, the fighter, and the hunter. Hobbes' theory of the state set forth from the perception that equality was fraught with danger to each from each, and hence to all from some:[12]

> ... when all is reckoned together, the difference between man and man, is not so considerable, as that one man can thereupon claim to himself any benefit, to which another may not pretend. ... the weakest has strength enough to kill the strongest, either by secret machination, or by confederacy with others....
>
> ... And therefore if any two men desire the same thing, which nevertheless they cannot both enjoy, they become enemies. ... if one plant, sow, build or possess a convenient seat, others may probably be expected to come prepared with forces united, to dispossess, and deprive him, not only of the fruit of his labour, but also of his life, or liberty.

Hobbes reasoned that all instruments of force must be yielded to one sovereign, an absolute ruler. But Americans were themselves already fugitives from conditions less repressive than those Hobbes advocated in *Leviathan*. The Hobbesian solution to the equality problem seemed inap-

[12] *Leviathan*, pt. I, chap. 13.

plicable, furthermore, because a whole continent appeared before the new American.

Was relocation rather than repression, then, the proper response to aggression? Herewith we encounter the "safety valve" and "virgin land" theses. This theme runs from Jefferson's celebration of an "empire of liberty" to the West, to be peopled by self-reliant yeomen and farmers; through Horace Greeley's exhortation to "Go West"; to Frederick Jackson Turner's hypothesis that the expanding frontier and free land formed the American national character.[13]

The land was there, pioneers took advantage of it, the population became restive and mobile. Yet these facts hardly justify the conclusion that movement was a satisfactory general solution to the problem of threatened security. Ethnographic research suggests a strong correlation between the competitiveness of a society and the importance of property both as an expression of "ego values" and as a means of achieving self-esteem and respect from others.[14] The fact that American society is both highly competitive and property-oriented is more than coincidence. The ability safely to stay put and enjoy one's acquisition was quite as crucial to realizing the American dream as was the freedom to pick up and go.

The frontier's usefulness as a safety valve was not inexhaustible. At some point roots went deep enough to hold. It was then necessary to have a means of insuring that the work of years would be safe from others who, by hypothesis, were unequal in achievement but on a par with their potential victim in ability to coerce or kill, and claim what was left. Law supplied this need, law that in the British tradition had always been the bulwark of property. Thus the framers' abiding—if not conspiratorial—concern for security of property supplied an element of continuity,

[13] See generally Frederick Jackson Turner, "The Significance of the Frontier . . ." in *The Early Writings of Frederick Jackson Turner* by E. E. Edwards (Madison, 1938), pp. 186ff., and Henry Nash Smith, *Virgin Land* (New York, 1950), esp. bk. III.

[14] Margaret Mead, ed., *Cooperation and Competition Among Primitive Peoples* (Boston, 1937, 1961), pp. 486ff.

linking pre-Revolutionary English law to the "basic doctrine" of American constitutional law.

The legal historian Maitland once observed that Britain's "whole constitutional law seems at times to be but an appendix to the law of real property."[15] This disposition made the inherited law especially useful to the "men of substance and property" who framed the Constitution and guided its early development. From the first, American constitutional law as a protection of property against the bogey of democratic predation energized public power to protect the value for which, in the Lockean philosophy, the state was erected in the first place. This disposition of law was functional. It appealed to the desire of every man whose efforts made him "more equal than others" to hold onto his gains. By bringing the community's weight behind the security of each individual's possessions, law provided a "ratchet effect." *What later became the heaviest burden imposed by legalism was, in the earliest days, its main advantage— namely, a sense of irreversibility of gains once secured.*

Legalism in America, then, emerged as a natural response to the problem of squaring equality of condition with inequality of achievement. Americans' regard for law must be explained functionally as well as historically—as something more than an erstwhile Englishman's inherited veneration for courts, judges, and laws. Law contributed to the achievement of a working syntax. It articulated readily with the ambient culture, which was materialistic and achievement-oriented and patronized by James' "bitch goddess, Success." Success in America meant that one could go up without fear of being pulled down; that properties gained would not be lost merely to the physically stronger, mentally more cunning, or morally less scrupulous. Law meant that equality might be the beginning of the story, but not the end, and the early lawyers' and judges' task was to develop the supremacy of law in those areas—especially security of property—where the radical threat was greatest.

[15] Frederic W. Maitland, *The Constitutional History of England* (1908), p. 538.

[3]

The Judicial Version of the Law Is Authoritative because Society Imputes to Courts as an Institution the "Rationalized" Wisdom that Simpler Societies Postulated of Leading Personalities

Sir Edward Coke, explaining to James I why that benighted sovereign should not take to dispensing the royal justice in person, gave classic expression to the tradition of law as a special province of lawyers: "Causes which concern the life or goods of his subjects are not to be decided by natural reason, but by the artificial reason and judgment of the law, which law is an art which requires long study and experience before that a man can attain to the cognizance of it."[16] Coke was referring to the common law as a body of complex and subtle rules built up over time by men—by the artificers of the law. The early jurists' task was similarly to convert "self-evident" principles into an equally artificial, equally technical, set of rules. Bagehot wrote that "the men of Massachusetts could work *any* constitution."[17] Much of the credit must go to those uncommon men united by common dedication to government by law and, in practice, to governing by legalism. Three names particularly stand out, those of Story, Kent, and above all Marshall.

Joseph Story served as Associate Justice of the Supreme Court for almost thirty-three years (1811-1844). During a third of this period, from 1829 to 1840, he commuted to Harvard as Dane Professor of Law. In his spare time Story tossed off weighty treatises—nine in all, ranging from *Bailments* (1832) to *Promissory Notes* (1845), and including the justly famed *Commentaries on the Constitution* (1833). Story was always a votary in the law's temple. Although regarded in his time as a master of expositional and forensic prose, Story found difficulty in communicating his feelings over the sublimity of the law. Necessarily, it was the prov-

[16] 7 Co. 63-65 (1609).
[17] Quoted in Edward S. Corwin, "The Progress of Constitutional Theory from the Signing of the Declaration . . . ," *Amer. Hist. Rev.*, 30 (April 1925), 511, 521.

ince of the tutored professional. Echoing Coke, Story asserted: "It is a system having its foundation in natural reason; but, at the same time, built up and perfected by artificial doctrines, adapted and moulded to the artificial structure of society."[18] Story fostered with all his eloquence the belief that law required a technical skill and intellectual mastery that denied laymen entry into its premises. Therewith went denial of access to some main levers of power in America's legalistic system.

Similar in disposition was Chancellor James Kent of New York. Kent's *Commentaries on the Constitution*, published over a four year period from 1826 to 1830, were in Blackstone's grand tradition and were destined to exert an influence on American law that was perhaps equally decisive. Kent's *Commentaries*, more perhaps than any other gloss on America's developing jurisprudence, inclined the law toward a private property bias. Like Story, Kent helped bring legal interpretation into the atelier of specialists, scattering allusions to ancient authorities throughout his work, invoking abstruse principles to justify opaque distinctions. Kent refused to reduce complex formulas to compendious principles that might have made law more accessible to the bumpkin country lawyers riding the swell of Jeffersonian and eventually Jacksonian democracy. Transmutation of the law into a specialized, mysterious craft seemed complete, or at least its success assured, in the defeat of David Dudley Field, leader of the codification movement in the 1840's.

Though John Marshall did little himself to develop the rationale behind juristic mystery, he turned the authority for judicial review, and thus premised the judicial check in the American governmental system, on the doctrine that judges alone are privy to the meaning and command of the law.[19]

Excepting only the vested rights doctrines which secured their places in American law, primarily at the state level,

[18] "Upon the Inauguration of the Author" (1829) in *The Legal Mind in America*, ed. Perry Miller (New York, 1962), p. 182.

[19] *Marbury* v. *Madison*, 1 Cr. 137 (1803).

through Kent's espousal in the *Commentaries*, virtually every central doctrine of constitutional interpretation from the formative period recalls first of all the name of Marshall. The list begins with judicial review itself, and includes next Marshall's correlative principle of judicial restraint—deference by courts to popular will as expressed in acts by politically responsible branches, especially the legislature.[20] Marshall's opinions in *Fletcher* v. *Peck* (1810) and *Dartmouth* v. *Woodward* (1819) elevated property to the highest plane, extending the sanctity of contract doctrine to public grants of land and to corporation charters.[21] In these areas Marshall's dedication to the buyer-seller model shows with particular clarity: for the determination of policy, reliance on the political check exerted through the franchise; and for the determination of private rights, reliance on free agreement formalized in contracts, whose sanctity it became the judiciary's high duty to maintain against all threat and jeopardy.

The doctrines of national supremacy enunciated in *McCulloch* v. *Maryland* (1819)[22] and *Gibbons* v. *Ogden* (1824) put the United States on its high road toward full political integration and material prosperity. But above all other contributions in its subsequent influence on the legal humour in America, was Marshall's doctrine in *Marbury* v. *Madison* (1803), that the Constitution is law in the sense of a body of rules to regulate behavior and (for present purposes, the crucial element) enforceable by judges. Thus Story, speaking to the apprentices of the legal trade at Harvard Law School in 1821, asserted: "The most delicate, and, at the same time, the proudest attribute to American jurisprudence is the right of its judicial tribunals to decide questions of constitutional law."[23]

The obscurantist tradition was not that of Coke, Story, Kent, and Marshall alone. Nor was it peculiar to England and America. Carl J. Friedrich and Morton Horwitz have

[20] *Gibbons* v. *Ogden* (1824), 9 Wheat. 1, 197.
[21] 6 Cr. 87; 4 Wheat. 518.   [22] 4 Wheat. 316.
[23] "To Members of the Suffolk Bar," in Miller, *Legal Mind*, p. 69.

pointed out that mystery and secrecy in folk ritual—and much of the judicial process in America is aptly characterized as nothing less than ritual—is often essential to the maintenance of an effective authority system. The examples are many and suggestive.[24] Thus Aubrey Richards has observed that among the Bamba of Rhodesia, "much of the tribal ritual is secret . . . and the advisory council is composed of what might be called an aristocratic caste." The parallels with the American judiciary are no less clear because the situation in America is not usually expressed quite so bluntly. If these "bakabila meet in sitting on the open ground of the capital . . . they use archaic language on purpose, so that the common people cannot understand."

Ritual is the very basis of authority among the Tikopia of Polynesia, who are the subjects of a standard work in ethnographic literature by Raymond Firth: "If a chief or elder imparts the last vestiges of his ritual knowledge to his son, then the gods regard that as a sign he is finished. . . . Only when he is very old or ill does he divulge the information." In ancient Thailand, Friedrich and Horwitz report, mystery and secrecy were so central that kings confiscated legal codes lest people learn what laws they had to obey, thus evacuating them of their authority.

If it is something less than a universal social law, the tendency to emphasize legal mystery nevertheless seems powerful and widespread. Some factor in the social syntax itself must be invoked to explain both the tendency toward mystification and the importance of the "mystifiers"—lawyers as a class.

Legal secrecy, moreover, seems at odds with the "fair-warning" value, discussed in Chapter II as a norm applicable to ruler-subject transactions. What the fair-play norm cannot by itself provide, but is fostered by a sense of arcaneness in the law, is order and stability. Mystery and ritual add to government's dignity. It is functional for law to be

[24] Carl J. Friedrich and Morton Horwitz, "Some Thoughts on the Relation of Political Theory to Anthropology," *Amer. Pol. Sci. Rev.*, 62 (June 1968), 536ff.

proof against uncontrolled individuality of interpretation and against whimsical change by those who see no barrier but their own will between themselves and the next new order of society. Some tendency toward mystery seems an inevitable by-product of the institution of law to insure order in society in the first place.

But if mystery seems inherent in law, how is the second step accomplished—the establishment of courts as the authoritative interpreters? Benjamin Cardozo in 1922 defined law as "a principle or rule of conduct so established as to justify a prediction with reasonable certainty that it will be enforced by the Courts if its authority is challenged."[25] E. Adamson Hoebel, the anthropologist who with Karl Llewelyn pioneered systematic study of primitive legal structures,[26] uncovered in the Cardozian formulation four elements, more or less generally found in legal systems from the most modern to the most primitive: (1) the normative element; (2) regularity; (3) enforcement; (4) courts.[27] We may translate the Hoebel categories to show how they parallel certain concepts advanced in the preceding analysis.

The proposition that law always contains a normative element corresponds to the idea that law facilitates performance of functions deemed desirable, either ethically or pragmatically, by those empowered to make authoritative judgments for society (which may vary from a small elite to broad consensus of all the people) in accordance with rules evolved to moderate the transactions involved in the function. The second element, "regularity," may be assumed to refer to consistency over time in the rules which look to predictability of behavior. This is necessary if behavior is to be institutionalized and harmonized into a coherent, functioning whole. Given law's efficacy, regularity of application helps insure predictability in areas of par-

[25] Benjamin N. Cardozo, *The Growth of the Law* (New Haven, 1924), p. 52.

[26] Karl Llewelyn and E. Adamson Hoebel, *The Cheyenne Way* (Norman, Okla., 1941).

[27] E. Adamson Hoebel, *The Law of Primitive Man* (Cambridge, Mass., 1954), p. 23.

ticular social significance. Such efficacy in turn depends in part on enforcement, the third essential element in Hoebel's list.

Hoebel's fourth element is "courts." Again, useful perspective may be given by the work of researchers in other disciplines—in this case, ethnography and psychology. Even in systems without formal, Institutional, courts, Hoebel argued, there almost always exist institutionalized means of resolving conflicts by recourse to some notion of right. "Right" is expressed in terms of the society's values, and the resolution is generally consistently performed by identifiable individuals. Such individuals apply the resolving formulas discussed in Chapter i. In fact they function as a court; they should be so accredited for analytical purposes.[28]

Applying data from experiments by the psychologist Muzafer Sherif, another anthropologist, Leopold Pospisil, pursued Hoebel's logic. In the Sherif experiments, as reported by Pospisil,[29]

> An individual was brought into a dark room [and shown a fixed, motionless point of light, but which because of the lack of reference appeared to move]. The same experiment was conducted with other observers. After this, the observers were permitted to tell each other their perceptions. . . . Thereafter they were asked to look at the dot once again and were told that this was done so that they could correct their observations and be more accurate. . . . The individual perceptions in the second trial tended to cluster in a narrow range, which was called by Sherif the group norm. . . . [T]he individuals within this "group norm range," who changed their original statements of observations very slightly or not at all, were functioning as persons with authority. The rest of the group were merely followers.

[28] *Ibid.*, pp. 22ff.
[29] In Paul Bohanan, ed., *Law and Warfare In Primitive Society* (Garden City, N.Y., 1967), pp. 26-28.

Friedrich and Horwitz, by similar reasoning, have quoted ethnographers against themselves, or rather against the claim that states lacking the easily recognizable Institutions of civil power for that reason lack any means of social control. Such a claim, advanced by Martin Gusiude in a study of the Yahgans of Cape Horn, seems to be refuted by Gusiude's own assertion:[30] "There are always certain . . . men, who as a result of their advanced age and blameless character, their long experience and mental superiority, have a moral influence of such importance that it amounts to positive control." Extrapolating from the work of Hoebel, Sherif, Pospisil, and Friedrich and Horwitz, one can deduce that law is not necessarily authoritative because it is enunciated by courts. Rather, *those who enunciate what on the empirical record qualifies as "law" constitute courts because they are authoritative.*

Courts in modern societies perform functions which in most primitive systems are carried out on an institutionalized basis by persons whose seniority, or whose endowment of blood or "mana," or whose special training or past attainments cause others to accept them as authoritative. Such persons both lead and enforce public opinion. A basic difference between primitive and developed systems is the greater articulation of functions in the latter.[31] Articulation results in rationalization—separate, more specialized and efficient performance by separate organs of the multiplicity of functions that a few organs, such as the family or clan, handle on a regularized basis in preliterate societies. In Chapter II, such organs were defined as Institutions.

Law-giving and law-interpreting are performed institutionally in some cultures by family heads or clan chiefs among many other functions (such as presiding over religious feasts and "rites of passage"; administering punishment; leading the tribe in battle). By what means do these

[30] In Friedrich and Horwitz, "Relation of Political Theory to Anthropology," p. 537.

[31] Robert MacIver, "Interests," *Encyclopedia of the Social Sciences,* 8: 144-148; Talcott Persons and Robert F. Bales, *Family* (New York, 1955), p. 9.

functions become in other cultures the peculiar province of a special Institution? How is the authority of the men who maintain the judicial institution changed into an authority attaching to the judicial Institution, so that the men filling Institutional roles are automatically permitted to share in the authority's potency regardless of their personal attainments?

Max Weber has shown that the very process of rationalizing functions can serve a legitimizing purpose.[32] In so-called rational-legal societies, articulation and apportionment of functions makes them "rational," and therefore largely justifies the transfer of authority from men acting institutionally to an Institution filled by men. Rationalization is socially useful. Through specialization and division of labor, it permits greater efficiency in the achievement of even a preordained (i.e., "imposed" or dictated) pattern of allocations. Moreover, in the case of courts, rationalization of functions emphasizes and regularizes the relative *exclusivity* of authoritativeness—the existence of a meaningful distinction between ruler and subject—which is logically required by the notion of order.

[4]

Court-Administered Justice, because it is Dependent on Appeals to the Public Sense of "Right," Requires a Coherent Public Sense Coupled with Public Respect for the Courts

The American predilection for converting questions of policy into issues of constitutional power, and issues of power sooner or later into questions of "right," seems closely associated with reliance on court-administered justice. It is fostered by the panoply and dignity characteristic of court procedure. Both the predilection and the procedure, moreover, reflect the weak Institutional position of the courts, at least as measured in terms of power.

One need not go so far as to accept the claim that the

[32] "Politics as a Vocation," in *From Max Weber*, ed. H. H. Gerth and C. Wright Mills (New York, 1958), pp. 77, 79ff. See also "Bureaucracy," pp. 196, 209-221.

American judiciary, possessing "neither purse nor sword," has no power whatsoever to admit that judges must look for backing to something beyond the coercive powers immediately available to them. Because of the courts' situation if for no other reason, the efficacy as well as the legitimacy of judicial utterances often depend on appeals to society's sense of "right." Such appeals both justify decisions and establish claims on the other branches to provide enforcement.

But the notion of such appeals as validators of law is not uniquely American. Every society possesses a bank of custom and usage reflecting accepted values and giving rise to accepted resolving formulas. Thus every society defers to some "higher law," if only by informally or even unconsciously confronting its positive legislation with a Law of Rules. As indicated, the requirement that a statute substantially conform with the rules often lies at the basis of the "test of reasonableness" as a measure of a law's validity, a subject which will be treated further in Chapter VI. Finally, every society develops institutionalized ways to determine breaches of law, essential custom, or higher morality. Such regularized procedures usually become Institutionalized by devolution on a determinate group of men, called judges, whose responsibility it is to insure the integrity of the institutions. The resulting Institutions are courts.

Judicial authority ultimately depends on two factors: first, the depth and extent of popular respect for courts as an Institution, a form of emotional capital on which judges draw for much of the effect of their utterances; second, the authoritativeness of the judges themselves as they are viewed by society's members apart from their Institutional positions. On these factors largely depends the probability that a judicial definition of what is "right" will be accepted by society. Once such acceptance has been gained, the basis is laid for the appeal that legitimizes the judicial decision and insures its enforcement. The judges themselves, because they are normally presumed to be "wise," are by the same sign presumed to define in terms of right that which is also helpful in society. By this fiction the judges presumably close the loop linking value with function.

But it is clear that judges in developed systems are presumed "wise" by Institutional imputation, analogous to the way that an officer in the army "becomes an officer and gentleman" by act of Congress, rather than by assertion of an empirically demonstrable fact. *When the fiction fails, so does the linkage of what is "right" with what is functional. And when the failure is found out, so is the defect in the rationalization on which a court's authoritativeness depends.*

It follows that society's constitution is not necessarily "what the judges say it is" at all. In any but a perfectly integrated society, there exist multiple centers of public opinion-formation. Some influencers of opinion take positions different from those espoused by courts. They then compete with the courts as sources of authoritative utterances regarding the limits and kinds of permissible behavior. These competitors' claims on society's support may, on some or all issues, exceed the courts' success in winning regard as society's authoritative law-interpreting Institution. The competitors too may undercut the judges' pretensions to special expertise as interpreters of the laws. When this happens, the authoritativeness of the competitive leaders of opinion is posed against the authority of the Institutional courts. Interpretations of basic norms issue from multiple sources with conflicting voices, producing dysfunctional results according to the definitions in Chapter II.

In such situations, the "laws," which are rooted in and reflect the rules, mediate least consistently and predictably between transactions and allocations. Such a situation of Institutional dispute (president versus Supreme Court), of conflicting authorities (Jackson and Taney versus surviving federalist judges), and of competing political values (majority rule versus private rights) emerged with Jacksonian democracy.

The model of society that informed Marshall's doctrines of political checks and sanctity of contract proved an inadequate template for the future. Free buyer-seller transactions, manifested in the political market through the ballot and in economic life through the importance of contract, became the basis of new and ultimately incompatible ruler-subject relationships: in the political arena, the growing power of democratic masses; and in the economic sphere, the growing power of those who controlled America's business life. Thus the early artificers' achievement yielded to a new variant of the same dichotomy, power of numbers versus rights of property, that had from the start contributed so signally to legalism in the United States.

[CHAPTER V]

TANEY AND
CONSTITUTIONAL *BRICOLAGE*

As was suggested in Chapter i, the judge is in the position of the *bricoleur* described by Claude Levi-Strauss in *The Savage Mind*—the position of a problem solver, usually one working on a project requiring special manual deftness because of the reduced scale of the operations involved. The *bricoleur* plies his craft, as do most judges, not by light of theoretical science but by a combination of intuition, experimentation, and acquired skill, and always within a received tradition, always making do with whatever tools and materials are on hand.

The constitutional document, together with the authoritative glosses on it, is at once a tool for resolving political problems and the material from which rationales for the resolving formulas must be fashioned. What Levi-Strauss wrote of the *bricoleur's* resources may be said of the constitutional clauses and precedents that constitute the judge's equipment for making decisions: "The possibilities always remain limited by the particular history of each piece and by those of its features which are already determined by the use for which it was originally intended or the modifications it has undergone for other purposes."[1]

The century following the death of Marshall in 1835 presented the American political system with some almost fatal shocks: the demands of Jacksonian democracy, slavery agitation and the Civil War, Reconstruction and the threat to separation of powers posed by the Johnson impeachment trial, industrialization and labor strife, the Great Depression. This chapter considers the Court's essay in constitutional *bricolage* in response to the first of these shocks. It discusses the formidable challenge, the narrowed jurispru-

[1] Claude Levi-Strauss, *The Savage Mind* (Chicago, 1962), p. 19.

dential resources, and the almost virtuoso performance of Marshall's successor, Roger B. Taney.

[1]

Jeffersonian and Jacksonian Democracy Struck Directly at the Legal Norms and Institutions on which the Federalist Syntax Was Based

"Sanctity of contract," long used as both a moral incantation and a judicial shibboleth, betokened the elevation of untrammeled buyer-seller freedom to the top of American political priorities. The opposing demand, associated with the Progressive movement, was that the Supreme Court give effect to "the power to govern," even at the cost of increased control over individuals. Already in the 1820's, American politics was feeling contrary pulls from the buyer-seller and ruler-subject models. Judicial defense of property, contract, and mercantile security was consistent with the dominance of the buyer-seller mode, was true to the philosophy of John Locke, and was in harmony with the leading federalists' economic interests. But since Jefferson's electoral victory over Adams in 1800, forces of populism had been contesting the federalist legacy. With Jackson's imminent occupation of the White House in 1829, the Jefferson tradition seemed finally to stand a good chance of complete success.

Yet federalists still manned the Courts. Federalist jurisprudence meant stability and permanence in a land where change was at least a philosophy, and for some, virtually a religion. Jefferson rejected the "dead hand" of the law. "I hold it self-evident," he wrote Madison, "that the earth belongs in usufruct to the living." Hence any generation's constitution and laws are "extinguished then in their natural course with those who gave them being. . . . If [these constitutions and laws] be enforced longer, it is an act of force, and not of right."[2] Jefferson fought a running feud with Marshall, whose *Marbury* v. *Madison* opinion had left no doubt about the federalist theory of the "permanence" of

[2] To James Madison, September 6, 1789, 15 Boyd 392, 396.

the Constitution. Jacksonians kept alive the Jeffersonian fear of acquisition of excessive power by an elite based on expertise in the "artificial reason" of the law. Yet such an elite, de Tocqueville perceived, had already risen to the status of an American aristocracy.[3]

Federalists emphasized the function of law as guardian of inequality of achievement. Jefferson's philosophical heirs stressed equality of opportunity. Jacksonians celebrated the planter and farmer, the mechanic and yeoman—celebrated them and worst of all, wanted to legislate for them. Justice Henry Baldwin, a Jackson appointee to the Supreme Court, summed up the national restlessness: "The history and spirit of the times admonish us that new versions of the Constitution will be promulgated to meet the varying course of political events or aspirations of power."[4]

The new aspiration was preeminently the Westerner's. America experienced a shift in its geographic center of gravity. Between 1810 and 1840, nine new states entered the Union, including Arkansas, Illinois, Indiana, Michigan, and Missouri. James Fenimore Cooper's Natty Bumppo—Deerslayer, Pathfinder, Leatherstocking, and all-purpose folk hero—personified the westward shift. As in art, so too in life. The frontier politico emerged, beginning with Jackson himself and including the hero of Tippecanoe, William Henry Harrison; Westerners like Davy Crockett, Thomas Hart Benton of Missouri, Henry Clay; and in the same tradition, Lincoln of Illinois. Self-made and self-assertive, the frontier leader seemed to vindicate the common man's ability to rule himself through governments locally designed and locally run, and assuredly best able to solve local problems.

Franchise reform in New York, Massachusetts, and Virginia shifted the political center of gravity. The nation approached universal white manhood suffrage. Elimination of property qualifications for the vote in Virginia occa-

[3] Alexis de Tocqueville, *Democracy in America*, chap. 16.
[4] Quoted in Edward S. Corwin, *John Marshall and the Constitution* (New Haven, 1918), p. 226.

sioned John Randolph's warning that if political power were divorced from property, power in the democratic masses would "go in search of property."[5] Federalists foresaw expropriation of the wealthy by the poor.

There was, finally, a shift in mood—a sense of freedom, deep-running, with a renewed conviction of boundless opportunity. De Tocqueville wrote of a nation "restless in the midst of abundance," and observed:[6]

> In the United States a man builds a house in which to spend his old age, and he sells it before the roof is on; he plants a garden and lets it just as the trees are coming into bearing; . . . he embraces a profession and gives it up; he settles in a place, which he soon afterward leaves. . . . Death at length overtakes him, but it is before he is weary of his bootless chase of that complete felicity which forever escapes him.

Mobility and material prosperity generated a revolution of rising expectations which fostered with equal inevitability an impatience with stability, with permanence, and with the pettifogging, crotchety values for which the Federalist jurisprudes had labored.

In this context Jackson's appointee and protégé, Roger Taney, acceded to the chief justiceship of the United States.

[2]

The Function of the Judiciary, when Passing on the Constitutionality of Statutes, is to Define the Limits of Policy as a Potential Limit on Individual Rights

Jacksonian localism confronted the constitutional nationalism inherited from Marshall. But in an important respect the Jacksonians' fear of national power was ironic. The early arguments favoring union assumed that "overbearing

[5] Summaries of the Franchise Reform Convention debates in A. T. Mason, *Free Government in the Making* (Oxford, 1964), pp. 408-440, esp. pp. 416ff. and 437ff.

[6] *Democracy in America* (New York, 1946), 2: 137, 136.

majorities" in the states held the danger of oppression.[7]
James Wilson asked in the Philadelphia Convention:
"Where must the people look at present for relief from the
evils of which they complain? Is it from an internal reform
of their Govt.? No. Sir, It is from the Natl. Councils that relief is expected. . . ."[8] "As to the destruction of State Governments," Hamilton wrote, "the great and real anxiety is to be
able to preserve the Nation from the too potent and coun-
teracting influence of these Governments."[9]

Marshall changed all that by his national supremacy decisions. But if Marshall had, to the consternation and con-
fusion of the anti-Federalists, expanded Congress's discretionary powers, he appeared to have done the opposite in
the field of private property-rights.

It will be helpful to refer to Fig. 1, which shows changes
in the range of discretion available to a legislature under a
particular constitutional limitation, say, that of the Contract
Clause.

Prior to judicial construction of the clause, the only limit
on a state legislature's authority to pass laws impairing
the obligation of contracts would be the legislature's own
fair interpretation of the clause. Let d, along the y axis, be
thought of as measuring this discretionary area within
which a legislature might, without overtly contravening the
applicable Constitutional clause, enact laws trenching on
contracts. Only the area outside the margins bounding d
would be completely secure, and therefore properly regarded as an area of indefeasible "rights."

Movement along the x axis indicates passage of time.
Contract cases will be brought before the courts, which will
pass on the legitimacy of specific legislative enactments.

---

[7] See Madison's argument in *Federalist No. 10*; also, generally,
Edward S. Corwin, "The Progress of Constitutional Theory Between
the Declaration of Independence and the Meeting of the Philadelphia
Convention," *Amer. Hist. Rev.* 30 (April, 1925), 511, esp. sec. 2 and
5.

[8] *Farrand*, 1: 355.

[9] To Col. Edward Carrington, May 26, 1792, Syrett, 11: 426, 443.

Fig. 1. *Rights and Discretion in Constitutional Adjudication*

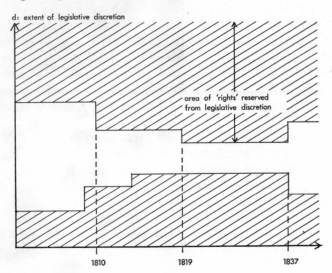

d: extent of legislative discretion

area of 'rights' reserved
from legislative discretion

1810   1819   1837

This the Marshall Court did, for example, in *Fletcher* v. *Peck*, and *Dartmouth* v. *Woodward*, which narrowed the discretionary area left to state legislatures. These decisions also expanded the area of "rights," increasing individual freedom to incur rights and duties by free agreement. Thus under Marshall constitutional law moved from the ruler-subject mode toward reliance on contract in the same sense in which the idea of such a modal shift, as the mark of allegedly "progressive societies," was first broached by Maine. And all that this progression implied in the way of restricting state powers adverse to the sanctity of exchanges freely agreed upon followed accordingly.

[3]
The Taney Court Reversed Marshall's Emphasis on Exchange in Favor of a Pragmatic Jurisprudence Giving Broad Scope to Legislative Policy

Taney was more or less openly commissioned by his patron, Jackson, to read into law the new tenets of grass-roots de-

mocracy, local prerogative, and popular government. But
it was the new chief's responsibility too, to keep the tradition of judicial *bricolage*. Himself a leader of the Maryland
Bar, and not always in his younger days an exponent of
Jackson's populist values, Taney was neither immune to the
"legal humour" nor insensitive to the need for stability.[10]

Yet how much stability could society take? Responding
to demands for public power to modify private interests,
even when secured by contract, for easy money to finance
economic growth, and for increased local prerogatives,
Taney fashioned what might be called a "political" conception of the Constitution. Constitutional interpretation would
respond to the politically dominant segment of society
rather than to received doctrines. The judicial check, originally thought of as a limit on political democracy, would
henceforth support the political check. Changes in the Law
of Rules—or more broadly, in basic mores, needs, and
values of society—must prevail over Rule of Law narrowly
defined. Taney eventually translated this conviction into a
principle of constitutional interpretation: "It will be regarded hereafter as the law of this court, that its opinion
upon the construction of the Constitution is always open to
discussion when it is supposed to have been founded in
error, and that its judicial authority should hereafter depend altogether on the force of the reasoning by which it
is supported."[11]

Taney's pragmatism appeared decisive in one of the first
cases brought to the High Bench under his presidency of
the Court. The facts leading to the pivotal *Charles River
Bridge* Case (1837) were as follows. Massachusetts char-
tered the Warren Bridge, to be built between Boston and
Charlestown, despite an earlier franchise to the Charles
River Tollbridge Company. After recoupment of its investment, the Warren Bridge would discontinue charging tolls.

[10] See esp. Gerald Garvey, "The Constitutional Revolution of 1837
and the Myth of Marshall's Monolith," *West. Pol. Quart.*, 18 (March
1965), 27, esp. sec. 2.

[11] *Passenger Cases*, 7 How. 283, 470 (1849).

The Charles River Bridge Company contended that a free Warren Bridge would impair remunerative traffic over its own bridge; and that Massachusetts, by chartering the new bridge, violated the Contract Clause.

Over a heated dissent by Story, Taney denied the older Charles River Bridge Company's right to exclusive service, claimed under Marshall's *Dartmouth* ruling.[12] The Court narrowed the range reserved from public interference. As suggested in Fig. I, it expanded the area of choice left to the state's discretion at the expense of individual freedom to determine rights and obligations by contract. The *Charles River Bridge* blow at contract sanctity, Story warned, struck at all entrepreneurial activity. Story contended vainly for the Contract Clause interpretation propounded by Marshall to maximize the security of rights and obligations incurred by individual agreement, and thus to strengthen exchange as a basis both of social interaction and mercantile development.[13]

But henceforth, Taney's opinion indicated, the state must not be reckoned merely an economic actor, free to bargain, contract, and exchange with individuals and groups. The state possessed both power and responsibility to insure society's larger interests. Public power must not merely enforce rights and obligations created in past buyer-seller transactions, but must impose conditions on those transactions. "Free exchange" pure and simple gave way to exchange subject to public power manifested through the Institutions of representative democracy.

Taney accomplished this ostensible reversal of Marshall's position without flagrant disregard of precedent. He worked within the inherited tradition. He displayed the high talents of a constitutional *bricoleur*. Indeed, Taney's casting about in the old Supreme Court reports turned up no fewer than four Marshall Bench opinions[14] in which doc-

[12] 11 Pet. 420, 549-550.
[13] 11 Pet. 420, 608.
[14] *Providence Bank* v. *Billings*, 4 Pet. 514; *Beatty* v. *Knowles*, 4 Pet. 168 (1830); *Jackson* v. *Lamphire*, 3 Pet. 289 (1830); *U.S.* v. *Arrendondo*, 8 Pet. 738 (1834).

trines had been advanced that could now be turned to service of the new constitutional jurisprudence. Taney cited, even quoted, the precedents, resting his argument particularly on Marshall's holding in *Providence Bank* v. *Billings* (1830). Manifestly, the Taney Court remade Marshall's fabric, but using Marshall's loom, and cutting with Marshall's tools—quoting passages from that judicial exemplar's own opinions. The justices helped maintain the form if not the substance of continuity in American public law.

Story again defended Marshallian orthodoxy, again without success, in *Briscoe* v. *Bank of Kentucky*,[15] the second of three cases normally thought of as comprising the "constitutional revolution of 1837." The Kentucky Bank had issued notes whose face value was payable by that bank on demand. Since the notes were intended to circulate as money, they apparently fell within Marshall's definition of "bills of credit" in *Craig* v. *Missouri* (1830).[16] Story urged that they were therefore illegal under Article II, Section 10. But the Court through Justice McLean reaffirmed *Craig*, citing Marshall's definition of bills of credit as "a paper medium, intended to circulate between individuals, for the ordinary purposes of society." Having paid this token respect to the "venerable and lamented Chief Justice," McLean dismissed Marshall's words as unhelpfully vague. He then upheld the Kentucky Bank.

In Story's view, the dismantling of *Craig* v. *Missouri* was an injury. But the Court's bland reaffirmation of *Craig* at the same time, coupled with citation of yet a second of his hero's old opinions to bolster the holding,[17] was more than an injury—it was an insult. Thus we find in *Briscoe* as in *Charles River Bridge* (and in the *Miln* Case, discussed immediately below) a strong disinclination openly to reverse received precedents. The Court's preference was to move in new directions, yes, but in the manner of the *bricoleur* rather than in that of the constitutional pioneer—by fash-

---

[15] 11 Pet. 257.
[16] 4 Pet. 410 (1830).
[17] Citing *U.S.* v. *Planters Bank*, 9 Wheat. 904 (1824).

ioning opinions to the extent possible from tools and material already available.

Mayor of New York v. *Miln* (1837) raised the question whether New York could require immigrants to register on their entry into the city under a municipal ordinance to protect against diseased, degenerate, or pauperized persons. Story objected that the act interfered with the national government's "plenary" power over commerce.[18] But the Court, ostensibly basing itself on *Gibbons* v. *Ogden,* upheld the New York act. The Court in effect gave the states freedom to carve up the "uniform whole" of American commerce through state-by-state legislation, at least so long as Congress refrained from passing laws preempting the states in any particular area. In *Miln,* the authority to regulate commerce was appropriated to state police powers. These, being no part of the national government's positive grants, were therefore "complete, unqualified and exclusive." The Taney Court thus laid the basis for laissez-faire decisions in the post–Civil War period which gave the bulk of power over interstate commerce to the states.

[4]

The Taney Court's Treatment of the Slave Issue—Especially in Dred Scott—Highlights the Extent of The Debt of American Constitutional Law to the Buyer-Seller Model

Sir Henry Maine observed that, in Roman law, the slave's inferiority was never so extreme as to put him wholly outside the slave-owner's family circle. His capacity to inherit was preserved, indicating that a slave was never viewed as mere property, but always as a human being. "The Roman law," Maine continued, "was arrested in its growing tendency to look upon him more and more as an article of property by the theory of the Law of Nature; and hence it is that, wherever servitude is sanctioned by institutions which have been deeply affected by Roman jurisprudence, the servile condition is never intolerably wretched." However, "under institutions founded on English Common Law" the

18 11 Pet. 102, 155-157 (dissenting), citing 9 Wheat. 193, 194.

legal categories afford "no true place for the Slave." The tendency, and in America the result, was to "regard him as chattel."[19]

The law's blindness to the personality of the bondsman furnishes a basis for distinction between pre-Emancipation Negro slavery and other forms of exploitation, including racial, that continued after the Civil War—a subject covered in detail in Chapter VI. In the former, the slave was but an object of buyer-seller transactions. In the latter, the "exploitee" is the disadvantaged participant in a ruler-subject relationship between himself and his employer. One learns in Kenneth Stampp's *The Peculiar Institution* (1956) and Stanley Elkin's *Slavery* (1959) of the pervasiveness of Southern law's dehumanization of the black man. The principal exception seems to have been, consistent with Maine's findings, in Louisiana—"least American of the Southern states," as Bancroft observed[20]—whose laws traced via the Napoleonic Code to the Romans. Legally, the word "chattel" in chattel slavery was no metaphor.

In the clash between humane values and economic function, the latter exerted dominant influence on the law. For the plantation system to work, and hence the economy based on that system and the society based in turn on that economy, the slave system had to be permitted to expand. Elkins observed: "The master must have absolute power over the slave's body. . . . Physical discipline was made virtually unlimited and the slave's chattel status unalterably fixed. It was in such a setting that those rights of personality traditionally regarded between men as private and inherent, quite apart from the matter of lifetime servitude, were left virtually without defense."[21]

Abolitionists despaired of change through evangelical appeals or moral pleadings. Needed was an increase in governmental power over slaveholders' vested rights in human chattel. In the *Dred Scott* Case (1857) Taney demonstrated

[19] Henry Maine, *Ancient Law* (London, 1924), p. 174.
[20] Quoted in Stanley Elkins, *Slavery* (Chicago, 1959), p. 54n.
[21] *Ibid.*, pp. 49-50.

how accurately abolitionists had appraised the situation. Society's dominant mode, so far as the theory of antebellum slavery was concerned, was the buyer-seller mode. This model gave little trouble as an organizing pattern for the Southern syntax as long as the fiction of the black man's impersonality was maintained as a tenet of law and an element of the political culture. The Negro might then readily be bought and sold as property. Once grant the Negro personality, however, the essential ruler-subject nature of the relationship between master and slave would become clear. No less clearly, abolition would require sufficient public power to permit government action on the slaves' behalf—public power at least coextensive with the sum of the individual power-relationships that obtained between each master and each slave.

Did the Constitution give such power? Taney said no—had said so years before the *Dred Scott* Case.[22] But on what grounds? As a constitutional *bricoleur*, Taney had to find a basis for slavery within the received judicial tradition. He had to justify the position ultimately taken in *Dred Scott* in terms of constitutional words and clauses which, though not determinant in themselves, would give access to less explicit elements of the political culture that were congenial to the slave interest.

The first requirement, in conflict with Taney's usual realism and pragmatism, was to maintain the buyer-seller rather than the ruler-subject model as the analytical basis of slavery's juridical defense. The black man's impersonality, his status as chattel, could be maintained as well. The real, if inexplicit, resolving formula having thus been vouchsafed by the buyer-seller model, the slavery argument might then be framed in suitable juridical terms. *The policy question—extension of slavery to the territories, let alone its standing within the already-slave states—thus cast in a form that raised an issue of constitutional power, could be settled by an appeal to rights defined in the Constitution's own explicit protection of property.*

[22] See *Groves* v. *Slaughter*, 15 Pet. 449, 508-510 (1841).

Taney's assertion in *Dred Scott* that Blacks "had no rights which the white man was bound to respect, and that the Negro might justly and lawfully be reduced to slavery for his benefit,"[23] cannot be understood out of the judicial context. The higher courts had continued under federalist dominance well into the mid-nineteenth century, most of them more concerned to stem Jacksonian legislation touching property than with abolitionist agitation. Judges loyal to Marshall's belief in the sanctity of property, seeking means to check democratic majorities, found a constitutional basis for enforcing their views as law in a New York Court of Appeals decision, *Wynehammer* v. *New York* (1856). There the court struck down a state liquor prohibition law, invoking the New York State Constitution's Due Process of Law Clause as a substantive, rather than merely procedural, limitation on legislative power.[24] Underlying *Wynehammer* was separation of powers, construed to prohibit retrospective legislation. By this doctrine, any act upsetting vested (i.e., pre-existing) rights was automatically held to be beyond the limits of legislative power.

The *Wynehammer* reasoning was transferred easily and directly to Taney's opinion in *Dred Scott*:[25]

An Act of Congress which deprives a citizen of the United States of his liberty or property merely because he came himself or brought his property into a particular territory of the United States and who had committed no offense against the laws could hardly be dignified with the name of due process of law.

As in *Wynehammer*, Due Process became a substantive barrier to legislation touching property, regardless of how unexceptionable might be the procedures used to protect the rights of persons affected by a law. What was property yesterday might not be taken away today. Such deprivation would be retrospective and, under Due Process, void.

The *Dred Scott* opinion well illustrates the thesis that

[23] 19 How. 393, 407.   [24] 13 N.Y. 378, 391-392.
[25] 19 How. 393, 450.

constitutional interpretation can be analyzed as an exercise in *bricolage*. An important difference between the *bricoleur* and the scientist, Levi-Strauss has observed, is that the former works with signs, the latter with concepts.[26]

Ideally, concepts discriminate between correct and incorrect beliefs about reality, but without any normative or "attitudinal" content. By contrast, signs always present themselves laden with meaning: with whatever normative, affective, and analytical content that culture has given them. The words of the Constitution are conventionally treated as signs, and were so treated when Taney construed them in *Dred Scott*. It was a certain cultural content of the Constitution's words, rather than any clear and compelling mandate in the words themselves, that Taney invoked on behalf of slavery.

What was wrong with *Dred Scott* was not that it used words to screen a decision made on other grounds—most judicial opinions, wittingly or not, do that. What was wrong was that those words reflected values rejected by most members of the society; reflected attitudes identified with a special, unrepresentative class and the Old South subculture; reflected benighted beliefs regarding the nature of slavery. *Dred Scott* was perhaps "correct" for the South because, with respect to the Old South, it was functional. But the same decision was not functional for U.S. society at large because it was incorrect.

[5]

Transcending Its Substantive Impact on Constitutional Development Was the Taney Court's Achievement of New Dimensions of Judicial Power and Choice

Taney died in 1863. He left a Court disgraced by *Dred Scott* and a personal reputation that remained largely in eclipse until it was rescued in the twentieth century by a sympathetic biographer, Carl Swisher. Yet Taney's achievements were real and lasting. From the Taney Court can be traced the expansive view of state powers, the basis of

[26] Levi-Strauss, *The Savage Mind*, pp. 18-20.

police legislation to promote the health, morals, and welfare of the people. In terms of the categories of power outlined in Chapter III, Taney moved U.S. public law toward a jurisprudence of "coercion and penalty." Buttressing the concept of police power, moreover, were intimations of a view of government associated with the political culture of Jacksonian democracy and at odds with both Puritanism and Utilitarianism. Emerging now was a view of public power as useful for the positive purposes of a good society, rather than as a necessarily repressive or inefficient force to be minimized.

The Taney Court's expansive police power concept, of course, also seemed a doctrinal invitation to fragmentation of national power by the states. This result, identified particularly with *Miln,* was reaffirmed in subsequent decisions passing on the legitimacy of state actions affecting interstate commerce.[27] Dual federalism interposed the power of individual states as an independent limit on the otherwise unobstructed "national political market," centering on the national electorate. In terms of this analysis, and Taney's conception of the Supreme Court as an Institution to insure the security of these state powers even against national policies having the apparent political support of the larger electorate,[28] we can interpret Edward S. Corwin's assertion that Taney substituted judicial supremacy for the principle of national supremacy.[29]

From the standpoint of Marshall's work, Taney may be appraised a moderator, a restorer of the balance toward less absolute interpretations of the scope of national power and the security of private rights. More, he institutionalized judicial freedom to reverse precedents while remaining within the limits of the judicial tradition; he maintained the appearance of continuity while achieving the substance of

[27] See *Licence Cases,* 5 How. 504 (1847) and *Passenger Cases,* supra.

[28] *Ableman* v. *Booth,* 21 How. 506 (1859).

[29] *Commerce Power* v. *States Rights* (Princeton, 1936), pp. 135-136.

change; he accommodated new problems with the received materials and tools—in all respects manifesting the skills of the constitutional *bricoleur*.

But in these respects too, while preserving and even strengthening legalism in the sense of court-centered resolution of policy issues, the Taney Court compromised legal irreversibility. The "ratchet function" discussed in Chapter IV seemed in danger. Ironically, the Court exempted itself from the very rule it sought to enforce against the legislature. Legislation must be prospective because this requirement is thought to implement a deeper cultural norm, a rule of fairness. But the same requirement logically should apply with equal force to *stare decisis*, since a court decision is regarded as much as a prospective delineation of the line between "rights" and "policy" as is any legislative enactment. If Marshall increased the area of rights reserved from legislative discretion, as depicted in Fig. 1, then the Taney Court by decisions contrary in effect to Marshall's appropriated to itself legislative discretion in the form of judicial freedom to decide a given case either way, basing the holding on pertinent earlier decisions. *Issues of legislative policy, having been converted to questions of constitutional power and "rights," were thus reconverted through the availability of divergent lines of precedent into issues of policy—but judicial rather than legislative policy.*

The Court, too, did more than merely shift from a jurisprudence emphasizing rights secured through free exchange, toward a "constitution of powers" liberating state legislative discretion from a narrow judicial definition of rights. By reversing direction in the law, the Taney Court opened new dimensions of judicial choice. In the laissez-faire era, Taney's successors made the most of the resulting opportunity.

[CHAPTER VI]

HELPING THE FITTEST
SURVIVE

THE CIVIL WAR's aftermath brought rich opportunities for material prosperity—opportunities, at least, for those with the vision, cunning, and strength to seize them. Improved technology, some of it produced by the war itself, opened new fields. There were the telegraph and the reaper, and prospects for economies of production through more efficient Kelly-Bessemer steel processing. The railroad's potential fired the entrepreneurial imagination. Populations moving West, plus the immigrant swell filling city rolls back East, stimulated growth. In 1865, the economy was waiting to catch up on deferred consumer spending, on plant retooling and expansion. The desire for post-war "normalcy" asserted itself. And normalcy after the Civil War, as some sixty years later, meant *business.*

[1]

Opportunities for Economic Growth Fostered a Political Philosophy Favorable to Large-Scale Exploitation of Natural and Human Resources

Business growth required capital accumulation, coupled with the ability to concentrate investments where and when opportunities for profit appeared. This need was met by corporate business organization, capable of issuing stock to acquire capital, and of converting financial and organizational energy into physical production at levels not achievable by small-scale effort. The flourishing of the corporate form in turn depended on a climate favorable to the acquisitive motive. It needed political stability to assure security of capital, plus reasonable prospects for fair returns on investments. A "safe" sovereign had not merely to refrain from expropriation or high taxes, but positively to pursue commercial and fiscal policies favorable to the acquisition and security of wealth.

A two-fold policy was indicated: first, the shackling of public power to minimize interference with activities calculated to advance business interests; second—and a frequently overlooked side of the laissez-faire strategy—the *expansion* of public power where needed to provide government with the authority to remove obstacles to efficient production, acquisition, and conspicuous consumption. An expansive interpretation of public power, seemingly inconsistent with the restrictions on government in areas directly trenching on business interests, justified the protective tariff, the liberal licensing of companies exploiting natural resources, and the use of troops to quell labor strife. Immigration quotas high enough to frighten right-thinking white Anglo-Saxon Protestants, and thereby to contribute to renascent nativist movements, provided the workers needed to lay a mobile population's tracks and to mine the nation's coal.

Economic growth usually requires a delay of consumer satisfactions, freeing resources for investment in heavy goods likely in the long run to yield greater returns. Short-term privation is the price of long-term growth. Every modernizing society has had to face, in its own way, this fact of economic life. What was the American way?

America's unexampled diversity of talents, always a source of inequity in the distribution of wealth, was coupled with an inequity almost as marked in the zeal with which different individuals enlisted in the righteous cause of moneymaking. The privations necessary for growth can rarely be spread equally even in a true egalitarian society. The tendency to diverge from such an ideal must be exaggerated in a society with a legal structure less than tender of those classes most likely to pay the heaviest price in sweat for growth. *The kind and degree of inequality needed to propel the U.S. to material prosperity commensurate with its physical potential was achieved by imposing economic power over those fated to be have-nots, keeping them in a state of deprivation which would insure the availability of their surplus product for the more compelling purposes of a society needful of large-scale capital accumu-lations.* It just happened, too, that these purposes were one with those of certain private persons—the haves.

Exploitation usually requires substitution of a ruler-subject relationship for the free buyer-seller transactions which predominate in a society based on exchange. This notion underlies the Marxian theory of exploitation, as well as interpretations of capitalistic imperialism built on Marx's thought.[1] The doctrine's implications have been stated by Franz Oppenheimer: "The moment when first the conquer-or spared his victim in order to exploit him in productive work was of incomparable historical importance. It gave birth to nation and state, to right and the higher economics, with all the developments and ramifications which have grown and which will hereafter grow out of them."[2] One need not adopt Oppenheimer's philosophy of history to ad-mit its relevance, or to perceive the usefulness of a theory of exploitation in interpreting Gilded Age America.

Less obvious is the usefulness of the patron-protégé con-cept. The Western mind characteristically posits a clear boundary between man and his environment. Florence Kluckhohn has thus described the typical Western attitude:[3]

. . . natural forces are something to be overcome and put to the use of human beings. We span our rivers with bridges, blast through our mountains to make tunnels, make lakes where none existed, and do a thousand and one other things to exploit nature and make it serve our human needs. In general this means that we have an orientation to life which is that of overcoming obstacles.

But man and his milieu may be viewed quite differently —as interacting in a single energy system. This system fol-

[1] See John Strachey, *The End of Empire* (New York, 1960), pp. 320-322.

[2] Quoted in R. M. MacIver, *The Web of Government* (New York, 1947), p. 15.

[3] "Dominant and Variant Value Orientations," in *Personality in Nature, Society and Culture,* ed. Clyde Kluckhohn and Henry A. Murray (New York, 1956), pp. 342, 347.

lows certain physical laws: "Neither matter nor energy can be created or destroyed"; "The tendency of thermodynamic processes is to increase the entropy or 'disorganization' of the system." Human behavior too is constrained to conform with these physical laws. Exploitation of America's resources (iron ore from the Mesabi; coal to reduce ore to steel; oil and gas; lumber; clean waters needed for many types of industrial enterprise) had to be preceded by inputs of physical energy in the right forms, sequences, and amounts (e.g., organic decay and geologic pressures, yielding oil) to produce and concentrate the resources in the first place.

From this standpoint, the entrepreneurs of America's Gilded Age took roles as protégés or parasites. Under laws favorable to exploitation of the physical domain, they converted into private profit resources initially produced at no cost to themselves but not without cost to the total energy system of which their own efforts were but the last chapter in a long biological-geological sequence.

As industrialism progressed entrepreneurs often assumed protégé roles in a second sense—for example, by locating plants near plentiful labor sources, close to pre-existing lines of transportation, or into jurisdictions particularly favorable to business. Though American industry was ostensibly erected on a laissez-faire interpretation of the buyer-seller relationship, every penny of profit included substantial increments derived from favorable participation in legally approved—but often, legally occluded—ruler-subject and patron-protégé transactions. U.S. culture invited, U.S. society accommodated, and U.S. constitutional jurisprudence ratified this development.

[2]

Guilded Age America Saw the Traditional Antinomy of Property v. Numbers Rationalized Anew in Terms of Social Darwinism

That great American morality play, "Survival of the Fittest," had a colorful cast playing to a large, appreciative audience. Judges proved increasingly adept at snatching

Rights of Property from threat of imminent ravishment by American constitutional law's stock villain, Power of Numbers.

Darwin's disciple, the English sociologist-philosopher Herbert Spencer, led Gilded Age intellectuals, pundits, and scholars in the mission of Darwinizing all knowledge, and thereby, all society as well. In Spencer's *Social Statics*, and largely because of the impact of his thought on late nineteenth-century political philosophy, two streams of political theory converged: the Utilitarian and the Puritan. Spencer stigmatized government as "essentially immoral." In words reminiscent of the Utilitarian optimist's hopes, he added that "as civilization advances [so] does government decay." The Puritan leaven afforded ample preparation for Spencer's view: "Magisterial force is the sequence of social rule, and the policeman is but the complement of the criminal. Therefore, it is that we call government a necessary evil."[4]

During a celebrated trip to the United States in 1882, Spencer helped install Social Darwinism in the American value and belief systems. Capping the tour at a farewell dinner in New York's fashionable Delmonico Restaurant, luminaries from business, letters, academic life, and even theology paid tribute to the man whose colorful titles— "The Man Versus the State," "The Sins of Legislators," "The Coming Slavery"—conveyed the message he brought from biology to politics.[5] Holmes scarcely overstated the position when he suggested that no other thinker in English of the age, save Darwin himself, exerted a more powerful impact on American thought.[6]

Major opinion-shapers of the day preached the gospel according to Spencer.[7] Charles Horton Cooley of the University of Michigan and Yale's renowned William Graham

4 "The Right to Ignore the State," *Social Statics* (1850).

5 For an account of the Spencer tour and Delmonico farewell dinner, see Richard Hofstadter, *Social Darwinism in American Thought* (Boston, 1955), pp. 48-49.

6 To Lady Pollock, July 2, 1895 in *Holmes-Pollock Letters*, ed. M. De Wolfe Howe (Cambridge, Mass., 1941), 1: 57, 58.

7 See Ralph Henry Gabriel, *The Course of American Democratic Thought* (New York, 1956), pp. 155-158.

Sumner, leading American sociologists and both authors of seminal works in their field,[8] avowed Spencer's sovereignty. Sumner wrote of the evolutionary struggle:[9] "The millionaires are a product of natural selection, acting on the whole body of men to pick out those who can meet the requirement of certain work to be done. . . . They may fairly be regarded as the naturally selected agents of society for certain work." Sumner's millionaires typified self-made success. Through such writings as the Horatio Alger novels, their figures became models to a generation. They exemplified Spencer's philosophy that "the fundamental law of social life" was the law of survival of the fittest.[10]

Spencer's proposition received active support from "the fittest" themselves. "The law of struggle," Carnegie wrote in 1889, "is here; we can not evade it; . . . and while the law may sometimes be hard for the individual, it is best for the race, because it insures the survival of the fittest in every department."[11] John D. Rockefeller testified to the law's universality, telling a Sunday school class: "The growth of a large business is merely the survival of the fittest. . . . The American Beauty Rose can be produced in the splendor and fragrance which bring cheer to its beholder only by sacrificing the early buds which grow up around it." This, said Rockefeller, "is not an evil tendency in business. It is merely the working-out of a law of nature and a law of God."[12]

These preachments contributed to the processes of social-

[8] See Charles H. Cooley, *Human Nature and the Social Order* (1902). This book's roots in Sumner's seminal work, *Folkways*, has been acknowledged at several points in both notes and text.

[9] William Graham Sumner, "The Concentration of Wealth: Its Economic Justification" (1902) in *Essays of William Graham Sumner*, ed. Albert Galloway Keller and Maurice R. Davie (New Haven and London, 1934), 2: 170.

[10] See Max Lerner's interpretive essay, "The Rise and Decline of the Titan," in *America as a Civilization* (New York, 1957), pp. 274-284.

[11] "Wealth," *North American Review*, 148, (1889), pp. 655-657.

[12] Quoted in W. J. Ghent, *Our Benevolent Feudalism* (New York, 1902), p. 29.

ization and acculturation, propagating the political culture of the Gilded Age. Industrial development required a shift toward a syntax patterned on the buyer-seller relationship. For a preponderance of society's members to support such a shift, it was necessary to underscore the importance not only of easily accepted values like "freedom," but also of the rightness, utility, and eventual social beneficence of the harshness that laissez-faire must portend. *If competition were to play its part in a self-executing cosmic design for progress, individuals must be left as free to suffer the consequences of failure as to enjoy the fruits of success.*

Thus Spencerian doctrines not only inclined their adherents toward limited use of negative state powers or sanctions, manifested in the idea that each person should have full latitude to pursue his own happiness so long as he did not interfere with the equal liberty of others (as in the old common law maxim, *sic utere tuo ut alienam non laedas*, now become a canon of constitutional interpretation).[13] Gilded Age political culture also implied a positive aversion to public assistance for have-nots, whose weakness or fecklessness would by such humane actions allegedly be rewarded. Such would have been contrary to the Darwinian aim of ruthlessly selecting out the least fit in the interest of the race. Social Darwinism, then, implied a specific theory of power. This theory both emphasized and rationalized a concept of the state as an instrument to invoke sanctions against wrongdoing, with a corollary denial of the legitimacy of services as appropriate forms of government action. Any proponent of public power might fear being labeled a socialist.

The two greatest threats to capital, at least as capital saw it, were the developing labor unions and the state legislatures. Higher American courts had reached the conclusion by the late nineteenth century that strikes for higher wages,

13 The classic source on this issue is Edward S. Corwin's "The Supreme Court and the 14th Amendment," 7 *Mich. Law Rev.*, 7 (June 1909), 643, passim.

shorter hours, or other direct economic benefits were lawful. But qualifications were evolved to limit the efficacy of this rule. A strike might be legal, yet picketing to support it might not be. Or a strike threat posing irretrievable damage to the goodwill of the employer's business—"good will" defined as property, and hence protected with special solicitude by common law standards[14]—might call forth injunctive relief to break the walkout before it even started. Inventive restrictions visited on such concepts as "fair competition," "illegal combination," "restraint of commerce," and the like narrowed the laborer's opportunities to escape servitudes resulting from economic want, and to develop the equality of power with employers necessary for meaningful buyer-seller bargaining on wages, hours, and work conditions.

Judge Holmes, then of the Massachusetts Supreme Court and dissenting in *Vegelahn* v. *Guntner* (1896), provided students of a later day the clearest perspective on the labor issue in the Gilded Age: "One of the eternal conflicts out of which life is made up is that between the effort of every man to get the most he can for his services, and that of society, disguised under the name of capital, to get his services for the least possible return. Combination on the one side is patent and powerful. Combination on the other is the necessary and desirable counterpart, if the battle is to be carried on in a fair and equal way."[15] It would take some forty years for Holmes' emphasis on fairness and equity—significantly, broached by that exemplar of explicit logic in judicial decisions as too patently a root norm to require justification—to become the touchstone not only of labor law, but of U.S. public law generally.

The premier legal talents of the day addressed themselves to the task of rationalizing a constitutional juris-

[14] See Charles O. Gregory, *Labor and the Law* (New York, 1946), pp. 141, 98, and Holmes' dissent in *Traux* v. *Corrigan*, 257 U.S. 312, 342-343 (1921).

[15] 167 Mass. 92, 108.

prudence restrictive of state powers. Thomas Cooley's *Constitutional Limitations* appeared in 1868, the year the Fourteenth Amendment was ratified. This famous volume helped in the eventual subordination of all state actions touching private rights to federal judicial scrutiny. Cooley's contribution to American jurisprudence paralleled and reflected Spencer's contribution to the political culture. As adept as Story and Kent had been in finding constitutional restrictions where none had been thought to exist before, Cooley equipped the courts with the doctrinal apparatus needed to circumscribe state powers over property. This shifted socioeconomic policy-decisions from the realm of expediency, to be decided by local legislatures, into the judicial arena. Here issues of power might be presented more starkly, and rights of property more reliably protected.

The Gilded Age juristic effort quickly found support in the new American Bar Association (founded in 1878), an organization Edward S. Corwin characterized as originally "a sort of juristic sewing circle for mutual education in the gospel of laissez-faire."[16] Its leading membership and most appointees to high judicial office—the two groups interlocked—had close affiliations with big corporations. The commentary on the resulting performance by Supreme Court Associate Justice Samuel Miller made good psychology and accurate history: "It is vain to contend with Judges who have been at the bar the advocates for forty years of railroad companies, and all forms of associated capital, when they are called upon to decide cases where such interests are in contest. All their training, all their feelings are from the start in favor of those who need no such influence."[17] It is indeed difficult to imagine a better example of the usefulness of the mental set concept than in the performance of America's Gilded Age judges.

[16] *Constitutional Revolution, Ltd.* (Claremont, Calif., 1941), p. 85.
[17] Quoted in A. T. Mason and W. M. Beaney, *American Constitutional Law* (Englewood Cliffs, N.J., 1968), p. 331.

The Supreme Court Wrote Laissez-faire into the Constitution Using Formulas Patterning the Law on an Essentially Unreal Buyer-Seller Model

The judicial *bricoleur*'s art was to use the available budget of cultural norms, constitutional doctrines, and legal precedents. With these he rounded out the Constitution's own bare words with a content congenial to the interests of commerce and the security of property. Laissez-faire entered the Constitution through formulas selected from a pre-existing tradition to permit entrepreneurs to exercise power over employees, both as individuals and as a class. Apparent freedom became actual servitude—but under the guise of, and ostensibly in accordance with, rules appropriate to judicial enforcement of fair buyer-seller transactions.

Laissez-faire jurisprudence drew its strength from the tradition of the state as an instrument of justice, limited by a higher political morality. Thus magisterial competence in the "artificial reason of the law" was transmuted with the shift to laissez-faire into a commission for judges to serve as society's moral theologians. As we shall see, this development not only affected the substance of constitutional law in the Gilded Age. It also seriously altered the Institutional balance, furnishing a basis for judicial assumption of ultimate authority to decide the reasonableness, and hence the constitutionality, of legislation.

Because of constraints on judicial choice grounded in respect for the written Constitution, protection of property had sooner or later to find lodgement in explicit words of the document. Laissez-faire could not rely indefinitely on the "spirit and genius of the system" as a bar to legislative action. The Fourteenth Amendment provision, "nor shall any State deprive any person of life, liberty or property without due process of law," offered the best opportunities. The Amendment was of recent date. The very vagueness of the words "Due Process" drew attention to the clause's potentialities. In 1905 Holmes protested that the Fourteenth

Amendment did not enact Mr. Herbert Spencer's *Social
Statics*.[18] Yet to a majority of his judicial brethren, there
seemed little question but that it had done just that.

In *San Mateo* v. *Southern Pacific Railroad* (1882), Roscoe Conkling, appearing before the Court, broached what
has come to be called the "conspiracy theory" of the Fourteenth Amendment. Citing a record of the Joint Congressional Committee that drafted the Amendment, on which
Conkling himself had served, he argued that in addition to
the obvious purpose of protecting Negro rights, the drafters
intended to secure universal respect for life, liberty, and
property, i.e., to protect corporations. He concluded that
the Amendment's framers used "persons" in the Due Process Clause to include corporations.[19] Conkling's argument
was facilitated by the fact that it was but a short step from
Marshall's definition of a corporation as an "artificial being,
invisible, intangible, and existing only in contemplation of
law" in *Dartmouth* v. *Woodward*[20] to the fiction of the corporation as a metaphorical person. Adoption of this metaphor endowed the corporation with a real person's rights—
and, of course, with the liabilities associated with the idea
of "personality" in the Anglo-American culture.

A high cultural value was attached to individualism and
self-reliance. Reflecting this, the American legal system
hinged on personal or individual liability both for private
delicts and public crimes. The concept of personal liability
was enlarged in decisions imputing individual personality
to corporations, with liability attaching thereto rather than
to the individuals comprising the company. Such verbal
legerdemain demonstrated the potential of the constitutional metaphor—treating an Institution (the business corporation) as if it were an individual, and applying to it
rules initially developed to regulate actual persons. In the

[18] *Lochner* v. *N. Y.*, 198 U.S. 45, 75 (dissent).
[19] 116 U.S. 138 (1883); and see Mason and Beaney, *American
Constitutional Law*, p. 329. See also Howard Jay Graham, "The 'Conspiracy' Theory of the 14th Amendment," *Yale Law Journal*, 47 (New
Haven, 1938), 371.
[20] 4 Wheat. 518, 636.

1890's the Court further enlarged the concept of corporation from that of a legal person with a specific, unique residence in a state to an economic enterprise still protected as a "person" by the Fifth and Fourteenth Amendments, yet unlike any person, existing not merely where its physical assets were located but wherever it did business.[21]

Central to the evolving judicial activism was the "test of reasonableness," traditionally a measure of the limits on judicial review of legislation. Historically, if a legislature's actions were "reasonable," it enjoyed a presumption of immunity from judicial second-guessing. What must be thought "reasonable" had been broached by Coke as an intellectual problem, to be solved by the "artificial" reasoning of the law. However, *whether a particular statute is "reasonable" is in fact usually a cultural, not a logical, issue.* The test does not merely turn on an ability to establish a discernible relationship between the goal of legislation and the means prescribed by the legislature to reach it. It turns equally on the conformity of the statute in question to norms prevailing in the society. Holmes emphasized that evaluative as well as cognitive elements entered into the reasonableness test:

> I think that the word "liberty" in the Fourteenth Amendment, is perverted when it is held to prevent the natural outcome of a dominant opinion, unless it can be said that a rational and fair man necessarily would admit that the statute proposed would infringe fundamental principles as they have been understood by the traditions of our people and our law.[22]

That courts owed deference to the legislature was inherent in the "clear case" notion that James Bradley Thayer, Professor of Constitutional Law at Harvard, advanced against growing judicial power in the 1890's.[23] And with

[21] See John Commons, "Value in Law and Economics," in *Law: A Century of Progress* (New York, 1937), 2: 336.

[22] Dissenting in *Lochner* v. *N. Y.*, p. 76.

[23] "The Origin and Scope of the American Doctrine of Constitutional Law," *Harvard Law Rev.*, 7: 129.

some exceptions—Taney's *Dred Scott* opinion is the obvious example—presumption of the constitutionality of legislation had remained the rule in federal courts till the last quarter of the nineteenth century. But in *Mugler* v. *Kansas* (1887) Justice John Marshall Harlan, in an opinion sustaining a state liquor prohibition law, warned that the Court need not take all legislative professions at face value:[24]

> There are, of necessity, limits beyond which legislation cannot rightfully go. . . . The Courts are not bound by mere forms, nor are they to be misled by mere pretenses. *They are at liberty*—indeed, are under a solemn duty—*to look at the substance of things*, whenever they enter upon the inquiry whether the legislature has transcended the limits of its authority. (Emphasis supplied.)

Then *Lochner* v. *New York* (1905) raised the question of whether New York State might regulate bakers' working hours. Justice Peckham for the Court admitted that liberty and property are alike held "on such reasonable conditions as may be imposed by the governing power of the state." Whence it followed:

> . . . when the state, by its legislature, in the assumed exercise of its police powers, has passed an act which seriously limits the right to labor or the right of contract in regard to their means of livelihood between persons who are *sui juris* (both employer and employee), it becomes of great importance to determine which shall prevail,—the right of the individual to labor for such time as he may choose, or the right of the state to prevent the individual from laboring, or from entering into any contract to labor, beyond a certain time prescribed by the state. . . .

Having introduced freedom of contract as pivotal, Peckham recited appropriate incantations against unconstrained legislative power.[25] In the instant case, individual liberty of contract might not be interfered with.

[24] 123 U.S. 623, 661.   [25] 198 U.S. 45, 56.

The *Lochner* decision signaled a new era in constitutional interpretation, one reflecting with particularly dramatic effect the impact of norms, beliefs, and attitudes altogether outside the ambit of public law in their original purport. The history of "liberty of contract" vindicates Holmes' call to study law as a record of the development and morphology of ideas. Crucial in this area, as in the post-1882 development of the law of corporations, was that of "personality." About the concept of personality, and linking it to the buyer-seller model, the judges erected an elaborate theory. The basic unit of economic transaction, and hence of society, was taken to be the individual, the "person"—and never mind whether that person be a lone worker among multitudes of industrial drones on an assembly line, or a major corporation impersonally hiring, employing, and firing hundreds of operatives.

This abstract person's characteristics, taken as the working assumptions of the legal rules formulated to regulate his behavior, were: equality in law; security in inequality of achievement in the sense discussed in Chapter IV; freedom of acquisition and alienation of property, including the worker's labor—and that of his children; and freedom of bargaining and contract, pointed out in Chapter II as an essential rule of most institutions patterned on the buyer-seller model. Of course, "freedom of acquisition" and "liberty of contract" between patent unequals in achievement meant freedom for the strong to dictate wages and hours; to dispose of employees' services; and to impose taxes on workers in the form of rents and sundry other economic servitudes imposed as conditions of employment.

Building on its free person doctrine, the Court achieved results similar to those of the *Lochner* decision, on the basis of similar reasoning, in *Adair* v. *U.S.* (1908)[26] and *Coppage* v. *Kansas* (1915).[27] By these decisions the Court felled federal and state laws that invalidated "yellow dog" clauses by which employees were required as conditions of employment not to join or to withdraw from labor unions. The

[26] 203 U.S. 161.   [27] 236 U.S. 1.

Court in *Adkins* v. *D.C. Children's Hospital* (1923) laid to rest a 1918 District of Columbia minimum-wage law for women and children.[28]

In enforcing liberty of contract the Court invoked the rhetoric of classical economics. Given a free market with free bargaining among individuals, the "fair" price of a good being exchanged—in this case, the worker's labor—would be set by market forces. However, individual workers did not have the economic staying-power, or even the freedom from immediate physical want, necessary to bargain as equals with their employers. *Adair* and *Coppage* inhibited the development of collective bargaining to provide equality of power on a class basis where it was missing on an individual basis. Judicial application of "freedom of contract" thereby masked capital's use of economic power to limit, not extend, workers' freedom. This dualism between the theory of free exchange in an open labor market, and the fact of legitimized exploitation, with capital and labor in the relative postures of rulers to subjects, persisted into the 1930's.

The Gilded Age, then, was marked by ritual devotion to the buyer-seller model as society's ticket to the millennium. This theory quite effectively occluded to the view of society's captains—its businessmen and its judges—the fact that most Americans found their legacy of political rights rapidly becoming a web of economic servitudes.

The free exchange rule also became formalized in Supreme Court pronouncements on the subject of rate regulation. Indeed, in this field the majority of instances of judicial negativism appeared.[29] In *Stone* v. *Farmers Loan and Trust* (1886), the Court had warned:[30]

The power to regulate is not a power to destroy, and limitation is not the equivalent of confiscation. Under pretense of regulating fares and freights, the State cannot re-

[28] 261 U.S. 525, 545.
[29] See Charles Warren, *The Supreme Court in United States History*, rev. ed., 2 vols. (New York, 1926), 2: 741.
[30] 116 U.S. 307, 331.

quire a railroad corporation to carry persons or property without reward; neither can it do that which in law amounts to a taking of private property for public use without just compensation, or without due process of law.

Thus interpreted, "due process" bore little resemblance to the ancient notion of fair procedure. Due Process now became a code word for the Court's determination substantively to revise the weighting of variables in the decisional model inherited from the Taney era. For while the legislature might constitutionally impose marginal restrictions or conditions on buyer-seller transactions, Due Process forbade it to act coercively. The *Stone* opinion when given full effect meant that the railroad could not be required to give service at any rate at which it would not provide the level of service in question under a contract freely arrived at. This was a new, difficult, and crepuscular test of Due Process. Nevertheless it prevailed well into the 1930's in the fields both of liberty of contract and regulation of rates.

Four years after *Stone*, in *Chicago, Milwaukee & St. Paul* v. *Minnesota*[31] the Court struck down the charter of the Minnesota railroad commission on the ground that it unconstitutionally deprived railroads of judicial review of rates set by the legislature. This case, pivotal in Supreme Court history for its assertion of substantive as opposed to procedural due process, has always been thought a remarkably sweeping assertion of judicial over legislative authority. "From that year," Charles Hough has written, "I date the flood."[32]

We have seen in Chapter v the importance of the model in the judicial mind during the process of selecting rules—often "modal rules"—to govern a particular class of transactions. By adopting the buyer-seller model and using it to screen the ruler-subject elements in the relation of master to slave, Taney appropriated an entire line of thinking to his decisional task in *Dred Scott*. Similarly, judicial acquisition

[31] 134 U.S. 418 (1890).
[32] "Due Process of Law—Today," *Harvard Law Rev.*, 32 (January 1919), 218, 228.

of supererogatory powers from the 1890's on reflected a duty imposed on the judges by their beliefs about the nature of society as much as a growing judicial appetite for power—indeed, rather the former than the latter. The Court's developing concept of Due Process may be viewed against a prevailing judicial model of the transactions involved (buyer-seller, rather than ruler-subject). The judicial versus legislative struggle was but a derivative manifestation of that model's implications. The rules invoked by the constitutional *bricoleurs* followed from the judges' model of the system, and the power struggle from the need to apply those rules.

Following *Chicago, Milwaukee & St. Paul* the Court could sustain legislation as "reasonable" or overturn it as violating Due Process, in either event supporting its opinion with respectable precedents to justify the holding.

[4]

Complementing the Laissez-faire Trend at State Levels, the Supreme Court Equally Successfully Immunized Business from Strong National Regulation

Following the turmoils in Europe of the 1840's and 1850's, the immigrant flood brought strong, willing bodies to America. It also brought "foreign" ideas, thus helping to coalesce middle-class opinion against labor. This xenophobic reaction had its counterreaction: development of a base for aggressive unionism.

In Homestead, Illinois, in 1895 a strike was called against the Pullman Railroad Car Company. A principal grievance had been George Pullman's refusal to reduce the rents that residents were charged in his company town to match recent reductions in the pay scales of Pullman's workers. Workers and residents, needless to say, were the same people. Pullman repeatedly protested his inability to see any relationship between his two roles as employer and landlord. In neither capacity did he see himself as other than an economic agent: a buyer of labor, a seller of occupancy in his "model town." Pullman never saw that his economic position gave him power. His control over workers' present wealth through payrolls, and over their future disposable income through debts and credits recorded in the ledgers of his company store, helped bring on the bitterest clash in an inglorious chapter of American history.[33] In *In Re Debs* (1895)[34] the Supreme Court through Justice David Brewer upheld a labor injunction against the Homestead strike, branding the workers' action an unlawful interference with the mails, since letters were commodities carried in Pullman cars.

In the name of liberty, courts by decisions such as those in *Adair, Coppage,* and *Debs* were in fact using power attaching to the judiciary to eliminate effective collective action on the economic front. In time the more resolute, the more ambitious, those Spencer called the "fittest," gained power through skillful use of economic leverage—in the generic sense, gained *political* power—in American society. Power over the so-called working class was legitimized by calling it precisely the opposite of what it really was, that is, by justifying it as the manifestation of free bargaining among men equal in law if unequal in nature.

Taxation, a power on which, frequently, all other governmental powers depend, furnished another area for defensive action against the power of numbers. The conservatives' effort climaxed in the renowned argument of Rufus Choate against the Federal income tax in *Pollock* v. *Farmers' Loan and Trust* (1895).[35] Accepting Choate's argument, the Supreme Court reversed a "century of error"— income taxes had been thought constitutional since *Hylton* v. *U.S.* (1796).[36]

Increasingly, observers felt that the Court functioned as a tool of capital against political democracy. In *U.S.* v. *E. C. Knight,*[37] another 1895 case, the Court further encour-

[33] The Pullman strike story is told fully in Stanley Buder, *Pullman: An Experiment in Industrial Order and Community Planning* (Oxford, 1967).

[34] 158 U.S. 564.

[35] 158 U.S. 601. See Choate's argument in 39 L. Ed. 1110.

[36] 3 Dall. 171.   [37] 156 U.S. 1.

aged this feeling. The Sherman Anti-Trust Act of 1890 had declared:[38] "Every contract, combination in the form of trust or otherwise, or conspiracy, in restraint of trade of commerce among the several states . . . is hereby declared to be illegal." Free competition, the Social Darwinist panacea, was thus enacted as a corrective to centralized economic power. But if the examples of Rockefeller and Carnegie taught anything, they taught that concentration resulted from free competition in the first place. The Sherman Act seemed to present an optionless choice between the Utilitarians' competitive market and consolidated markets which, with the American Beauty Rose, vindicated Spencer's law of "survival of the fittest."

The Court responded by blinking the inconsistency in the theory of self-perfecting competition, with the effect of removing the consequent embarrassment of the Sherman law. E. C. Knight & Company had long dominated America's sugar industry, making it a prime target of the Sherman Act. In a stroke of hermeneutic inspiration, the justices reasoned in an opinion by Chief Justice Fuller that "commerce" referred only to transportation. Products could not be transported until they were produced. But in the *Knight* case the sugar was produced within Louisiana. The producing company was therefore not liable to congressional control under the Commerce Clause. The Knight Sugar Trust was exempt from prosecution under the Sherman Anti-Trust Act.

Finally in *Hammer* v. *Daggenhart* (1918)[39] the Court struck down a Federal law prohibiting passage in interstate commerce of articles produced with child labor, arguing over a vigorous Holmes dissent that the Child Labor Law trespassed on powers reserved to the states under the Tenth Amendment. The *Hammer* decision brought national power under the Commerce Clause to perhaps its narrowest dimension, and at a time when industrialization made regulation increasingly necessary. "Stubborn theory con-

[38] 26 U.S. Statutes 209 (chap. 647).
[39] 247 U.S. 251.

quered pliable facts."[40] The Court established the rights of children to freedom of contract in a society theoretically dominated by buyer-seller relationships on as high and sacred a level as the similar "freedom" of their fathers.

During the chief Justiceship of William Howard Taft, 1921-1930 inclusive, thirteen federal laws were struck down in the famed "carnival of unconstitutionality."[41] The Court was committed to business beliefs and values in a business culture, impartially restricting power touching property from whatever source. The old resolving formulas flourished. Unions threatening free exchange found judicial power arrayed against them. In *Truax* v. *Corrigan* (1921)[42] the Supreme Court strengthened the injunction as an anti-strike weapon by five to four. In another labor case, *Bedford Stone* v. *The Stone Cutters' Association* (1927),[43] Taft again joined four of his Supreme Court brethren in upholding an injunction designed to break a sympathetic strike. The Court struck down state laws falling outside narrow areas deemed legitimate for public action in *Wolff* v. *Court of Industrial Relations* (1924).[44] And four years after *Hammer* v. *Daggenhart*, in *Bailey* v. *Drexel Furniture* (1922),[45] it said that taxation could not be used to regulate child labor indirectly, since such regulation was itself prohibited by the *Hammer* decision. *Hammer* and *Bailey* together set up the Court as censor not only of the types of activity in which Congress might engage, but also of the means Congress could employ and even the purposes to which its explicit powers might be put.

The upshot was that the Court created a zone of no power:[46] Congress was strapped by restrictive interpretations

[40] Morris Cohen has written: "Facts are more pliable than stubborn theories. Facts can be ignored, explained away, or denied. But theories are mental habits that cannot be changed at will." Quoted in Mason and Beaney, *American Constitutional Law*, p. 339.

[41] Statistics in Henry Abraham, *The Judicial Process* (Oxford, 1968), p. 292.

[42] 257 U.S. 312.   [43] 274 U.S. 37.

[44] 262 U.S. 522.   [45] 259 U.S. 20.

[46] This notion was first developed by Edward S. Corwin. See his *Commerce Power v. States Rights* (Princeton and London, 1936).

of the Commerce Clause and the Tenth Amendment, and the states were even more severely limited by Due Process requirements under the Fourteenth Amendment. A safe zone for business was created in which neither nation nor states could act. This zone of no power was preserved on the fiction that restriction of public power automatically served free exchange in capital, resource, and especially labor markets. In fact, the judiciary primarily maintained the power of business to manage and allocate the nation's resources—almost the very definition of political power advanced in Chapter II—in the interest of national economic development.

CHAPTER VII

THE LIBERATION OF
THE STATE

THE ERA from Melville Fuller's accession to the chief justiceship in 1888 till the New Deal saw two contradictory lines
of precedent. One line of decisions, reflecting traditional
American values of "rugged individualism" and freedom
from restraint, had a laissez-faire orientation. The second
line responded to the functional needs of an industrial society, and justified increasing government involvement in
its citizens' affairs. This tension between value and function,
and its eventual resolution in a new constitutional jurisprudence, are the subjects of the present chapter.

[1]
*The Demands on Government Posed by a Complex Indus-
trialized Society Portended a Shift in Political Philosophy,
from a "Sanction" to a "Service" Orientation*

Large-scale industry which developed under laissez-faire
raised anew the American "problem of bigness." Distrust
of bigness, tracing through the Jefferson-Jackson fear of
concentrated power, reflected the general concern of a generally conservative people lest power of any sort grow to
excessive proportions. But hard-headed Americans had
learned too that bigness had a cash value. Concentration
translated into profits, especially if it meant control of markets and prices. Enterprise on an imperial scale could
achieve unprecedented efficiencies. Development of trusts,
of holding companies and of the corporation's protected
legal position, facilitated necessary capital accumulations,
stock manipulation, coordination of operations, and concentration of industrial know-how.

Bigness carried emotional rewards as well as economic
benefits, as in the "conspicuous consumption" treated with
devastatingly sardonic effect by Thorstein Veblen in *Theory*

of the Leisure Class (1898). Bigness also signified moral achievement. The winning of an industrial captaincy proved its possessor's success in the Darwin-Spencer struggle. A further perspective on the place of materialistic competition in American culture came from Max Weber's thesis that Calvinistic Protestantism fostered striving for visible, material success, since prosperity could be taken to signify election to spiritual salvation.[1]

Cultural beliefs and attitudes favored industrial bigness. What then of government bigness? Progressives questioned whether development in the one sphere did not require—and hence justify—correlative expansion in the other. How might America's energies be liberated for public purposes from a constitutional jurisprudence formed by framers jealous and fearful of government, and developed by theologians of laissez-faire? The Civil War had shown that government could, and on occasion must, function as more than a passive night watchman protecting property rights. But for government to do appreciably more than this, while still satisfying the terms of its buyer-seller "contract" with the people, would require revolutionary changes in popular attitudes.

We have seen that much of the history of American public law can be summarized in terms of the simultaneous or alternating application of two theories, the Puritan and the Utilitarian. Both theories saw the individual as primarily responsible for his own well-being, either on moral grounds or on the basis of a test of efficiency. And the attitudes toward government particularly associated with Puritanism emphasized law's deterrent, retaliatory, and coercive aspects, its reliance on sanctions to control would-be wrongdoers. This negativism found echoes and reflections throughout the American political culture—not least in a strong bias toward restraining and limiting the powers of the state. The competing view of the state envisioned a broader charter for public action, especially in the cate-

[1] Max Weber, *The Protestant Ethic and the Spirit of Capitalism* (1906).

gories labeled "bribery" and "reward" in Chapter III. Progressives called for provision of positive services to citizens satisfying certain conditions of need, circumstance, opportunity, or behavior.

The federal government had precedents for such services as promotion of scientific research and collection of technological data. The Smithsonian Institution, the Weather Service, and the Census Bureau among others proved the value of the acquisition and dissemination of useful information by the government. By the 1862 Morrill "Land-Grant College" Act, and by laws establishing academies at West Point and Annapolis, the government vindicated its role as sponsor and participant in the educational field.[2] "Pork barrel" public works projects had long been a staple of American legislative politics. But such precedents, however suggestive of dormant federal powers, scarcely decided federal authority to undertake massive social and economic welfare activities.

Every new federal service would cause government to obtrude further into the lives of the citizenry, increasing its leverage over society's allocations of values and—worse—increasing government's ability to impose coercive sanctions under the guise of services.[3] So it seemed on the eve of the New Deal.

[2]

The New Deal Replaced the Buyer-Seller with the Ruler-Subject Mode as the Dominant Social Model, Responding to Seriously Inequitable Allocations of Wealth and Power in U.S. Society

What factors led to the shift in the allocation of values such as power and wealth that had resulted from "free" buyer-seller transactions under judicial protection of "liberty of contract" and similar rules? We may discuss this issue using the framework developed in Chapter II.

[2] See generally Don K. Price, *Government and Science* (Oxford, 1962), chap. 1.
[3] The most important exploration of this theme is in Charles Reich, "The New Property," *Yale Law Journal*, 73 (April 1964), 733.

Social transactions, we have seen, give rise to a Law of Rules prescribing the manner in which the various modes of interaction "ought" to be carried out—although this does not mean that every rule is tied to a particular mode, or that the four modes discussed in Chapter II exhaust the distinctions that would have to be made for a satisfactory "theory of society." If the rules do their job—helping to regularize behavior patterns, making them predictable and "expected" —then they by definition generate institutions. Such institutions, in the sense of regularized conduct, are frequently reflected in concrete, and often in official, organs of society: the institution of ritualized giving is reflected in charitable Institutions; regularized practices of trucking and trading are manifested in the Institutions of business—firms, markets, and the like.

Courts are official Institutions for orderly resolution of disputes by individuals appealing to some higher and (to the layman) inaccessible source of "right." In any society, and through any of a wide range of law-finding techniques from privileged communication with spirits to study of a written constitution, courts utter authoritative statements of certain portions of society's rules. If society's coercive potential is ultimately available to back up such statements, these may properly be called "law."

Reflecting its source in, or at least consistency with, the rules, law seeks to insure that allocations of value in all areas with respect to which it speaks are in accord with those rules. This was termed the "mediating function" of law in Chapter II, and brings us back to the idea of law as conservative, back to the idea of culture and society articulating with each other, back to the relationship between transactions and allocations with which society as a behavioral phenomenon is at bottom concerned.

Allocations result from transactions. Transactions in turn are responses to existing allocations. Thus, whenever an individual assumes or even tries to assume a role as a buyer, seller, ruler, or patron he is entering or seeking a transaction to alter society's existing allocation of values, however marginally, in his favor. Conversely, a donee is profiting by someone else's response to an allocation which induces that "someone else"—the donor—to perform an act of generosity.

Unlike the individual who has a large enough share in the existing distribution of wealth to enable him to purchase food, a starving man is more likely to steal his next meal (a ruler-subject transaction) than to purchase it. The donor-donee mode and its characteristic virtue of generosity often dominate in societies marked by severe scarcity of resources—among the Nuer of arid East Africa, for example, and among the Eskimos, where the practice even extends to loaning of wives. In such contexts, sharing literally becomes a key to survival.[4] And it is an insight dating at least to Aristotle[5] that inequity in the distribution of wealth is a chief source of revolutionary ferment—that is, of agitation to alter the existing pattern of allocations through force.

We may apply this framework, and the interplay of transactions and allocations implicit in it, to the situation of American public law at the start of the repression. The Supreme Court had come to be widely viewed as the main gear in an Institutional apparatus devoted to preserving inequities of wealth achieved through reliance on the buyer-seller model. Yet the prime vehicles to facilitate flow of money within the established buyer-seller network were in collapse. Hoover left office "to the sound of crashing banks." By Inauguration Day, thirty-eight states had closed their banks. The remaining ten were restricting their operations.[6]

National income had fallen more than 50 percent from the pre-1929 figure; farm foreclosures and business failures hit an all-time high. In Minnesota, where in 1932 half of all real property was mortgaged, a farmer named Blaisdell tried to pay off a note on his land. Price levels had dropped to half, and farm prices to nearly one-fourth, of the values

[4] See E. E. Evans-Pritchard's studies of the Nuer, and Walter Goldschmidt, *Man's Way* (New York, 1959), p. 158.

[5] *Politics* (Jowett), 1236-1237.

[6] William Leuchtenberg, *Franklin D. Roosevelt and the New Deal* (New York, 1963), pp. 38-39.

prevailing when Blaisdell's debt was incurred. Faced with widespread discontent and some violence, the Minnesota legislature unanimously approved a statute authorizing courts to provide temporary relief from payments. Blaisdell sought to take advantage of the law. His mortgagor charged that it violated the Constitution's Obligation of Contracts Clause.

A narrowly divided Court through Chief Justice Hughes sustained the debt moratorium.[7] Hughes based the Court's opinion on what might be termed a theory of economic functionalism. He stressed the unity of the U.S. economy and its need for harmonious working of parts: "Where in earlier days, it was thought that only the concerns of individuals or of classes were involved . . . it has later been found that the fundamental interests of the State are directly affected; and that the question is . . . of the use of reasonable means to safeguard the economic structure upon which the good of all depends." Hughes observed that it was unrealistic to think in terms of rights and duties rigidly prescribed through agreements among individuals. Public power was needed to supply supporting ruler-subject guarantees against default and disorder "by virtue of which contractual relations are worthwhile." The Minnesota Moratorium decision recalled the similar theory advanced by Taney in *Charles River Bridge*. Eventually Hughes' thesis of interdependency, generalized to apply to society as a whole rather than merely to the economy, would underlie the Supreme Court decisions upholding the New Deal.

Four justices dissented—Butler, McReynolds, VanDevanter, and the conservative spokesman, Sutherland. Sutherland's dissent was cogent, ill-humored, a fine example of metaphorical thinking. Metaphorical thinking facilitated direct application of the Law of Rules to such abstractions as states and legislatures, as in attempts to urge rules of individual thrift on governments. "A family cannot spend more than it earns, nor can a government" is an analogy

[7] *Home Bldg. and Loan Ass'n.* v. *Blaisdell*, 290 U.S. 398.

still heard from those who deplore deficit spending in the
public sector.[8] Sutherland applied rules of personal thrift
with truly Puritan certitude to the case at hand. "The present
exigency is nothing new," he asserted. "The vital lesson
that expenditure beyond income begets poverty, that public
or private extravagance, financed by promises to pay, either
must end in complete or partial repudiation or the promises
be fulfilled by self denial and painful effort, though constantly
taught by bitter experience, seems never to be
learned. . . ."[9]

Hughes and the majority saw the issues not as moral but
utilitarian questions. What needed protection were not
absolute Puritan values but specific interests of the parties.
Hughes cited the disparities of size, interest, and staying-
power of the parties involved. The mortgagors throughout
the state were "predominantly corporations" as compared
with the individuals faced with loss of homes and liveli-
hoods. The finance corporations' main concerns, wrote
Hughes, were "reasonable protection of their investment
security," and those of the individuals, ability to keep their
property. The Moratorium, by contributing to the social
order on which all else depended, came closest to reconciling both interests.

Two months after Minnesota Moratorium, the Court further evidenced an intent to supplant laissez-faire concep-
tualism with pragmatism. *Nebbia* v. *New York*[10] tested a
state legislature's right to fix retail milk prices. Discarding,
as James Beck expressed it, the "precedents of fifty years
without even the decency of funeral obsequies,"[11] the Court
rejected the liberty of contract doctrine as a five to four
majority though Justice Roberts upheld the New York
Milk Law.

Response to the Court's handiwork was immediate and

---

[8] See esp. Alvin Hansen's *Fiscal Policy and Business Cycles* (New
York, 1941), chap. 10, sec. 1.
[9] 290 U.S. 398, 471-472 (dissent).
[10] 291 U.S. 502 (1934).
[11] Quoted in E. S. Corwin, *Constitutional Revolution, Ltd.* (Claremont, Calif., 1941), p. 76.

for the most part enthusiastic. The *New Republic* predicted that "the Supreme Court sees no unconstitutionality in the Roosevelt program."[12] Alpheus T. Mason summarized reactions to the 1934 brace of cases: "It is almost inconceivable that a majority of the Court will set aside any substantial legislative effort to deal with an emergency which Justice Brandeis characterized as 'more serious than war.' "[13] These expectations would be cruelly rewarded in the event. By demonstrating that they could permit extraordinary exercises of power, the justices revealed their ability to forbid. The hand that gave approval could, with equal finality and unpredictability, take away.

[3]

The Supreme Court, Reversing its Early "Liberal" Outlook, Invoked the Classical Principles of Separation of Powers and Dual Federalism against the New Deal

The so-called Gold Clause Cases of 1935[14] tested the constitutionality of repudiation by the United States of the gold clause in government bonds. The repudiation was narrowly upheld, adding to hopes that the New Deal could count on solid five-justice support. The Gold Clause Cases threw into sharp relief the relationship between the judicial model of the transaction involved and the resolving formulas which would be employed to regulate those transactions and to settle disputes arising from them. These cases also highlighted the split between liberals and conservatives over the relationship between morality—or more generally, the Law of Rules—and law in the formal sense.

The ability to redeem public bonds on terms assumed binding as between seller and buyer went to the heart of any relationship of trust between government and the investment community. The most stringent rules of the buyer-seller transaction seemingly applied, especially if, assisted

[12] T.R.B., January 24, 1934, p. 307.

[13] "Has the Supreme Court Abdicated?" *Amer. Rev.*, 238 N. (October 1934), 353, 360.

[14] *Perry* v. *U.S.*, 294 U.S. 330.

by metaphorical thinking, the government were conceived of as having rights and obligations similar to those of any other financial transactor. Even the majority felt that the repudiation was therefore immoral and unconstitutional, yet refused to decide that bondholders were entitled to sue for reimbursement.

The judicial mind would continue to puzzle observers, as it had in its Gold Clause reasoning—but not, as in the Gold Clause decision, to the comfort of New Dealers. In 1935, on the ground that the wall between legislative and executive power had been breached by excessive delegations of authority from Congress to the President, the Court struck down the "hot oil" provisions of the National Industrial Recovery Act in *Panama Refining* v. *Ryan*,[15] and then in *Schechter* v. *U.S.*—in a sweeping blow at the most sweeping New Deal act—struck down the NIRA itself.[16]

The NIRA, symbolized by the Blue Eagle, sought to coordinate the entire national productive capacity through interlocking production and sales codes drawn up jointly by government and industry. As Thurman Arnold later put it, "A mandate went out from the White House through all the land that every industry should go up to Washington and be coded."[17] The Act's grandiose conception counted against it, for NIRA dramatized the plight of the individual confronted by Big Business now holding hands with Rooseveltian Big Government, subjecting him willy-nilly to Big Codes and Big Trouble if he disobeyed. In their briefs against the New Deal, leaders of the Bar stressed an appeal to the traditional American aversion to bigness—an aversion effective at the emotional, if not always at the rational, level.

The NIRA also threatened the traditional American fealty to localism. Sir Josiah Stamp, visiting the United States at the time of the *Schechter* case, remarked on the emotional attractions of state sovereignty. From American attitudes, as much as from the standing of states' rights in legal

---

[15] 293 U.S. 388 (1935).　　　[16] 295 U.S. 495 (1935).
[17] *Fair Fights and Foul* (New York, 1964), p. 50.

theory, derived its potency in constitutional interpretation. Stamp observed that though conditions required "Washington to act on an embracing and comprehensive scale in economic affairs, yet the idea of a transfer of State rights to the Federal Government meets with every kind of psychological resistance. . . . [In] such matters the average mind in the States is as old in its outlook as the Constitution itself."[18]

Finally, NIRA ran counter to separation of powers by granting the president wide discretion to approve and enforce the codes. For a unanimous court, Hughes rejected the government's "attempt to justify action which lies outside the sphere of constitutional authority." He termed the NIRA an unconstitutional delegation of "coercive . . . lawmaking power" to the executive. Countering an argument invited by his own economic functionalism in Minnesota Moratorium that the Depression required a response of unusual dimensions to break the cycle of interrelated economic failures, Hughes answered: "Extraordinary conditions do not create or enlarge constitutional power. . . . Those who act under [constitutional grants] are not at liberty to transcend the imposed limits because they believe that more or different power is necessary." Hughes then preached a Tenth Amendment sermon over the Blue Eagle's carcass: "If the commerce clause were construed to reach all enterprises and transactions which could be said to have an indirect effect upon interstate commerce, . . . the authority of the State over its domestic concerns would exist only by the sufferance of the federal government."[19]

Scholars ridiculed the justices' distinction between direct and indirect effects. "They point to a process more mechanical than any that can give wise results in the world of human affairs," Thomas Reed Powell of Harvard charged. "One objection . . . is that they speak with the tongue of physics rather than with the tongue of economics."[20] But the

[18] Quoted in E. S. Corwin, "The Schechter Case—Landmark, or What?" *N. Y. Univ. Law Quart. Rev.*, 13 (January 1936), 151, 153.
[19] 295 U.S. 495, 528-529, 546 (1935).
[20] "Commerce, Pensions and Codes II," *Harvard Law Rev.*, 49 (December 1935), 193, 208.

Court had more than common sense or even economic awareness on its side. It had support in U.S. political culture for "limited government," embodied as an ideal in separation of powers, and for the Jeffersonian belief in localism against accretions of power in Washington. Both sentiments supported the *Schechter* decision. Both sentiments happened also to be supported by a growing feeling that NIRA's code structure had been sloppily executed on a faulty design by inept social tinkerers: doomed as unfunctional if not as illegal.

Again invoking the Tenth Amendment, the Court in *Carter* v. *Carter Coal* (1936) struck down the Guffy Bituminous Coal Act regulating wages and hours in a hopelessly depressed mining industry.[21] Arguing that coal production was reserved to regulation by the states, Justice Sutherland for the majority asserted: "Extraction of coal from the mine is the aim and the completed result of local activities," perhaps on the theory that miners take coal home and eat it for dinner. However extensive, the coal industry's impact on interstate commerce was "secondary and indirect." An allusion to Hughes' resolving formula from *Schechter* disposed of the Guffy Act: "The distinction between direct and indirect effects of intrastate transactions upon interstate commerce must be recognized as a fundamental one, essential to the maintenance of our constitutional system."

Schechter had suggested that the Commerce Clause was a broken peg, but Congress's authority to tax and spend for the "general Welfare" remained by and large unchallenged by restrictive judicial construction.[22] Interest centered on prospects for the Agricultural Adjustment Act, the New Deal's experiment in taxing and spending as a means of crop control. This Act laid a processing tax on middlemen in commodity trading. With proceeds of the tax, farmers could be paid various amounts in exchange for promises to limit crop acreage. In *Butler* v. *U.S.* (1936) the Court

21 298 U.S. 238 (1936).
22 This was the thesis of Corwin's *Twilight of the Supreme Court* (New Haven, 1934). See esp. chap. 4.

through Justice Roberts called the plan an invasion of "the reserved rights of the states. It is a statutory plan to regulate and control agricultural production, a matter beyond the powers delegated to the federal government."[23] Though ostensibly decided on grounds of dual federalism, *Butler* in fact brought into play more basic issues of American political culture.

Roberts had made his philosophy clear in the earlier Railroad Retirement Case (1935).[24] There, for a divided Court, he struck down a workers' pension plan as based on "the contentment and satisfaction theory." Roberts could not then find a constitutional support for the service state. Nor could he in *Butler*, in part on the ground that, by offering farmers benefits if they would take crops out of production, the AAA exerted a forbidden kind of power:[25]

> The regulation is not in fact voluntary. The farmer, of course, may refuse to comply, but the price of such refusal is the loss of benefits. The amount offered is intended to be sufficient to exert pressure on him to agree to the proposed regulation. The power to confer or withhold unlimited benefits is the power to coerce or destroy.

In *Butler*, questions of a kind conventionally styled "constitutional" were ostensibly crucial: does the General Welfare Clause permit spending for general as opposed the specific purposes? Does the Tenth Amendment prohibit entry by the national government into the agricultural field? But Constitutional clauses, though useful for formulating issues in an accepted idiom to raise their standing under the "Supreme Law of the land," frequently are not precise or narrow enough to dispose of substantive issues once they are thus formulated. The political culture, of which judges serve as agents, must then decide.

Behind the federal questions in *Butler* were more basic

[23] 297 U.S. 1, 68 (1936).
[24] *Railroad Retirement Board* v. *Alton Railroad Co.*, 295 U.S. 330 (1935).
[25] 297 U.S. 1, 70-71.

theoretical issues. Indeed, the federal structure, so far from being the "given" in that case, hinged on the Court's answers to broader and deeper questions. Is "bribery" as defined in Chapter III a legitimate exercise of public power? Was the AAA's inducement to crop reduction an element of buyer-seller bargaining between government and farmer, and hence voluntary? Or was it an unjustified ruler-subject transaction whereby Big Government exacted involuntary behavior of the little individual planter? Is it permissible to think of public power as an instrument of an expansive service program, rather than as an always suspect, always repressive agent of social sanctions?

[4]

The "Constitutional Revolution of 1937" Sustaining the New Deal under Threat of F.D.R's Court-Packing Laid the Basis for the Contemporary American Service State

Roosevelt had been in office four years now, and had seen his program eviscerated by a Court seven of whose members had been appointed by conservative Republican predecessors. An eighth, McReynolds, though a Woodrow Wilson appointee, proved most reactionary of all. By mid-1936 twelve New Deal measures had been declared unconstitutional.[26] Bold legislative measures were needed, and the Court-Packing plan certainly was that.[27] Roosevelt announced the proposal on February 5, 1937. By the President's plan, a Supreme Court justice could resign at seventy. If he refused to do so within six months after his birthday, the president would have authority to appoint an additional, presumably a younger and more forward-looking, justice in his place. The nine justices, in open court when a page handed each a copy, impassively scanned Roosevelt's assurance that the proposal would expedite the Court's proceedings.

[26] See pt. II, U.S.S. Hearings on S. 1392, 75th 1st, pp. 205-210.

[27] For the chronology and development of court-packing see Gerald Garvey, "Edward S. Corwin and the Court-Packing Plan: Scholar in Politics," *Princeton Library Chronicle* (Winter 1970), pp. 1-15.

To amazed reporters, Roosevelt justified the plan as conservative of "our form of government." "[I]f these measures achieve their aim," he told Congress, "we may be relieved of the necessity of considering any fundamental changes in the powers of the courts or the Constitution of our government."[28] The Roosevelt revolution must be far-reaching in effect, but subtle in execution. Change the substance, preserve the form!

Yet the proposal struck at both substance and form. The emotional and symbolic strength of the judiciary as a quasi-religious Institution surfaced. New Deal opponents allied with erstwhile presidential supporters to stop F.D.R.'s flank attack on the Court. After hearings on the Court plan the Senate Judiciary Committee asserted: "The only argument for the increase which survives analysis is that Congress should enlarge the Court so as to make the policies of this administration more effective."[29] As the ancients did cry "Great is Diana," their uproar filling all Ephesus (Acts 19: 23-41), so did Americans, seeing F.D.R.'s assault on the temple of their laws, raise the cry—"Great is the glory of the Supreme Court," and their protest was broadcast over the land.

The feeling that F.D.R. acted guilefully, claiming merely to have advanced a measure to expedite judicial administration, fueled emotional support for the Court. Yet the New Deal team was now in Congress, however momentarily restive and recalcitrant. The Court was in real danger. The result, as most observers interpreted it, was the Court's "switch in time that saved nine"—when three 1937 cases overturned past decisions under the Fourteenth Amendment, the Commerce Clause, and the Spending Power.

By February 1937, the Court had decided, but not yet announced, a liberal result in the Washington Minimum Wage case. *West Coast Hotel* v. *Parrish*[30] overruled *Adkins* v. *Children's Hospital* on its face. Hughes, for a five

[28] *New York Times*, February 6, 1937, p. 8.
[29] *Adverse Report of the Senate Judiciary Committee.*
[30] 300 U.S. 379 (1937).

to four majority recurred to the economic functionalism of his Minnesota Moratorium opinion. He underscored the interdependency of the economic and the political, of free exchange and effectively exercised public power, noting that constitutionally protected liberty of contract can in reason include only "liberty in a social organization," not liberty *instead of* a working social organization. Hughes recognized that apparent bargaining freedom had become actual power to impose servitudes on employees: "The community is not bound to provide what is in effect a subsidy for unconscionable employers." The alternative to public power was not freedom for all. It was private power—and, Hughes wrote, "The community may direct its law-making power to correct the abuse which springs from their [unconscionable employers'] selfish disregard of the public interest."

Some thought the *West Coast Hotel* about-face portended favorable decisions on national power. On April 12, in an opinion sustaining the Wagner Labor Relations Act, the Court appeared to prove the optimists correct. *NLRB* v. *Jones & Laughlin*,[31] though a victory for the New Deal, had equivocal long-range implications. Because the administration could not really be sure that the Court had conceded defeat in its war against the New Deal, neither could it afford to give an inch in the Court-Packing campaign. F.D.R. pushed ahead. Meanwhile the Government prepared to defend the Social Security Act in the case which would tell whether the promise of *Jones & Laughlin* was genuine.

By the 1935 Social Security Act Congress had required employers of more than eight workers to contribute to a central fund. Annuities would be paid to enrolled members if they satisfied specified employment or age qualifications. In *Steward Machine* v. *Davis*, responding to the argument that the Act was a "soak the rich" scheme serving no legitimate constitutional purpose, Justice Cardozo replied for a five-justice majority: "It is too late today for the argument

[31] 301 U.S. 1, 37 (1937).

to be heard with tolerance that in a crisis so extreme the use of the moneys of the nation to relieve the unemployed and their dependents is a use for any purpose narrower than the promotion of the general welfare."[32]

The Act had a second provision whereby employers would receive up to 90 percent credits from the nation for taxes paid into a federally-approved state unemployment scheme. The record speaks eloquently regarding this stipulation's effect on the states. In 1931 only Wisconsin had unemployment compensation. On the vigil of the federal Act's passage California, Massachusetts, New Hampshire, and New York passed laws of their own—with the provision, in Massachusetts' case at least, that state provisions would take effect only if the federal law were passed or at least eleven of her industrial rivals passed similar acts. After 1935, with the federal Act on the books, thirty-eight additional states got on the Damascan route to social justice by passing laws of their own.[33] The law's assailants argued that after the nation took the first step, the states had no alternative but to follow. They were coerced into passing unemployment laws. If so, the Act usurped reserved state powers and was unconstitutional. This contention had some considerable force if appraised within a dual federalism framework that interposed the very existence and independence of the states as limits on national power.

As in *Butler* v. *U.S.*, a leading constitutional issue turned on the theory of federalism. Again, the drawing of the line between national and state powers would depend on the Court's theory of the nature of government. Such a theory would be grounded in norms and attitudes regarding the "sanction" versus the "service" orientation. Cardozo for the majority met the conservatives' argument in just these terms. He disdained to decide the point through talismanic allusions to the Tenth Amendment. "The difficulty with petitioner's contention is that it confuses motive with coer-

[32] 301 U.S. 548, 586-587 (1937).
[33] Charles Curtis, *Lions Under the Throne* (Boston, 1947), pp. 177ff.

cion," Cardozo wrote.[34] Those categories of power termed
"bribery" and "reward," which had been struck from the
national government's constitutional resources in *Butler*,
would not henceforth be denied on the basis of antecedent
theories of governmental propriety. The constitutional basis
of the service state, hinging on the nation's ability to influence behavior by manipulation of inducements rather than
through inposition of sanctions, was secure.

[5]

The New Deal Shifted Constitutional Law from Reliance
on the Buyer-Seller Model to Dominance of the Ruler-
Subject Mode in Expanded Public Power on a National
Scale

The New Deal climaxed a long standing conflict between
value and function in American constitutional law. The 1937
decisions resolved the issue in favor of a jurisprudence
tailored for an integrated industrial society, though this result conflicted with Lockean values of private rights and
personal property as the bedrock of political morality. Furthermore, the New Deal fostered—and was in turn supported by—basic changes in American political culture.
These included shifts in popular attitudes toward the
proper role and scope of government (e.g., sanctions versus
services) as well as in beliefs about the operation of U.S.
politics and Institutions (e.g., realistic versus metaphorical
modes of analysis). Inevitably, these changes had an impact
on the Court's role. The principle of judicial restraint,
marking a new Supreme Court deference to Congress's
judgment on social and economic legislation, recognized in
practice what American political theory had required from
the first: that the primary control on government is political, exerted through the ballot box, with the judicial
check intended merely as an auxiliary.

The New Deal and the changes it forced in U.S. public
law reflected the natural and, in the circumstances, predictable reaction of society to a situation felt by a preponder-

[34] 301 U.S. 548, 589 (1937).

ance of its members to be one of unnecessary and worsening inequity. By the early 1930's, inequities in wealth and power had brought many close to the point of outright revolution.[35] The New Deal gave substance to popular determination, under the motivation of existing skewed allocations of value, to shift from the buyer-seller mode to dominance of ruler-subject relationships manifested in expanded public power exerted on a national scale.

Yet even after the Social Security Cases, extensive mopping up was necessary. In *U.S.* v. *Darby* (1941),[36] an at last unanimous Court through Justice Stone burned all dual federalism bridges. Stone labeled the Tenth Amendment a "mere truism" that interposed no barrier to national action. In *Darby* and the cases leading up to it, the Court went far toward outright elimination of constitutional limitations on government action in the social and economic spheres. The old forms—and with them, the primacy of the old forms—were gone.

What would be put in their place?

[35] See the discussion of the appeal of revolutionary figures by Arthur Schlesinger, Jr. in *The Politics of Upheaval* (Boston, 1960), pp. 15-211.
[36] 312 U.S. 100.

CHAPTER VIII

TOWARD A
NEW POLITICAL SYNTAX:
BEYOND *BRICOLAGE*

THE FRAMERS' anti-statist political culture required that power be limited or, where not limited, at least made private and screened from view. Using forms associated with the buyer-seller mode, the framers and their successors occluded essential power relationships. For while the ruler-subject transaction assumes inequality of the actors, the buyer-seller relation postulates—even where it does not achieve—open results freely arrived at through rational decision-making by at least putative equals.

In 1937 the Supreme Court stopped functioning as a political magic wand, propagating the illusion of nonexistence of power. The service state liberates public power to serve positive, constructive ends, and the buyer-seller model gives way to candid recognition of the ruler-subject relationship's dominance. Authoritative allocations of value are increasingly made through exercises of public power—especially through "bribery" and "reward" (and by national rather than local power at that), instead of through agreements among persons freely interacting as "buyers" and "sellers."

A change in attitudes accompanied the coming of the service state. Such change does not occur quickly or without strain. "Individualism" and "liberty" are still identified with the market orientation. They are often thought to be hallmarks of a society marked by free buyer-seller relationships. As discussed in Chapter VI, this view was central to the moralistic laissez-faire of William Graham Sumner, Horatio Alger, and the industrialists. Whether "individualism" and "liberty" can be realized, and if so to what degree, in a society honeycombed with ruler-subject relationships that (by definition) constrain free choice is a central challenge to post-1937 American political theory.

[1]
The Post-1937 Preoccupation with First Amendment Freedoms has been in the Tradition of Bricolage

A variety of means may be employed to facilitate articulation of interacting legal and cultural elements to develop a new political syntax. Certain of these means—the techniques of cultural *bricolage*—have figured importantly in the preceding analysis. We have seen, for example, how metaphorical thinking, used as a basis for transferring norms in one area to an often quite different area, contributes to the achievement of syntax by promoting consistent, even replicative, patterns in both areas. By this technique, as we have seen, courts applied concepts and rules of personality to corporate enterprise. By metaphorical thinking "fiscal conservatives" regularly appeal for enforcement of certain rules of household economy, such as balanced budgets, in the quite different field of government taxing and spending. Metaphorical thinking has also had an important part in the development of post-1937 constitutional jurisprudence.

Perhaps no doctrine better illustrates the transfer of rules evolved to moderate buyer-seller relationships to an essentially alien field than does the "marketplace theory" of free speech. This theory holds the ultimate test of an idea to be its ability to survive in competition. The marketplace theory reflects a predisposition among economists, and especially among those who espouse free exchange on ideological grounds, to rely on competition as a means of ensuring "quality" not only in goods and services as traditionally understood, but quality in ideas as well.

Jefferson believed that truth armed with its natural weapons—free speech, discussion, and debate—could conquer error. "If there be any among us who would wish to dissolve this Union, or to change its republican form," he said, "let them stand undisturbed as monuments to the safety with which error may be tolerated where reason is left free to combat it."[1] The same idea found eloquent expression, cast explicitly in terms of the economic model, in the opinions, especially the dissents, of Brandeis and Holmes—the latter believing that the "best test of truth is the power of the thought to get itself accepted in the competition of the market."[2]

Certain basic rights bear an essential relationship, both logical and empirical, to the political process, now recognized as dominant over the judicial check. Without free speech and information, political democracy would be crippled, the electorate uninformed. Justice Cardozo expressed this view in *Palko* v. *Connecticut*: freedom of thought and speech "is the matrix, the indispensable condition, of nearly every other form of freedom."[3] Such freedom seemed the prerequisite of a political system founded on consent. It was as necessary to enlightened choice at the ballot box as was the counterpart of protected free speech, free bargaining among buyers and sellers, necessary to competitive improvement of products in the marketplace.

The marketplace doctrine underlies what has come to be called the doctrine of political restraints, adumbrated in Justice Harlan Stone's controversial footnote four in *Caroline Products* v. *U.S.* (1938). In *Caroline Products*, the principle of presumption of the constitutionality of legislation, in the absence of a clear showing to the contrary, was invoked to uphold a statute against a charge of illegal trespass on property rights. Stone's law clerk, Louis Lusky, inserted a footnote in his draft of the justice's opinion for the Court: "Different considerations may apply, and one attacking the constitutionality of a statute may be thought to bear a lighter burden, when the legislation aims at restricting the corrective political processes, which can ordi-

[1] First Inaugural Address, March 4, 1801.

[2] See esp. Holmes, joined by Brandeis, in *Abrams* v. *U. S.*, 250 U.S. 626, 630 (dissent).

[3] 302 U.S. 319, 327 (1937).

narily be expected to bring about repeal of undesirable legislation."[4]

Lusky's draft expressed the marketplace theory. It argued that specific freedoms—speech, discussion, open elections, assembly—deserved a higher place by virtue of their special relation to the political processes. These freedoms might take precedence even over the public will, at least in the sense that their jeopardy would reverse the presumption of constitutionality of popular legislation. Lusky's draft led the Court straight back to the pre-1937 controversy over the proper scope of judicial power, not least because of its reliance on the old form of judicial reasoning setting forth from buyer-seller assumptions.

The central machinery of representative government was the free and open ballot. Political restraints were primary. Exemplifying anew the primacy of form, Lusky sought to protect the procedural integrity of democracy, not to assert any preferred place for speech over other constitutional values on the basis of disparities in their intrinsic merits. The function of free speech thus conceived was that envisioned in the classical, rationalistic buyer-seller model that is shared by democratic and economic theory.

Stone revised and expanded Lusky's draft. He put three new conditions on the presumption of constitutionality where his clerk had suggested only the one deriving from the marketplace theory:[5]

There may be narrower scope for operation of the presumption of constitutionality when legislation appears on its face to be within a specific prohibition of the Constitution, such as those of the first ten amendments, which are deemed equally specific when held to be embraced within the Fourteenth. . . .

It is unnecessary to consider now whether legislation which restricts those political processes which can ordinarily be expected to bring about repeal of undesirable

[4] Alpheus T. Mason, *Harlan Fiske Stone* (New York, 1956), p. 513.
[5] 304 U.S. 144, 152, footnote four.

legislation, is to be subjected to more exacting judicial
scrutiny under the general prohibitions of the Fourteenth
Amendment than are most other types of legislation. . . .

Nor need we inquire whether similar considerations
enter into the review of statutes directed at particular re-
ligions . . . , or national . . . , or racial minorities . . . ,
whether prejudice against discrete and insular minorities
may be a special condition, which tends seriously to cur-
tail the operation of those political processes ordinarily
to be relied upon to protect minorities, and which may
call for a correspondingly more searching judicial
inquiry.

Stone's revision hinted a scope of judicial activity more
far-reaching than was implicit in the political restraints
doctrine.

The first of the three conditions suggested for special
judicial scrutiny of legislation might be termed the "condition of literalness." This condition, which subsequently became associated with the libertarianism of Justice Hugo
Black, turned on the explicit mention of certain rights in the
first eight Amendments. This first condition might give
absolute protection to freedom of speech and of press, because both are explicit in the Bill of Rights. But it would
exclude altogether freedom of demonstration which, however necessary in some cases to give effect to free speech,
is unmentioned in explicit terms in the Bill of Rights.[6] Second was the doctrine of political restraints, which viewed
the judiciary as but an auxiliary check in the U.S. system,
yet one charged with special responsibility to maintain the
integrity of the political process. Stone's third or "discrete
and insular minorities" condition foreshadowed the Court's
developing sensitivity to minorities' rights against what
Madison in *Federalist* No. 10 had called "interested and
overbearing" majorities. So stood Stone's three-point doc-

[6] Justice Hugo Black's clearest discussion of his libertarian phi-
losophy is in the recorded television interview, "Justice Black and the
Bill of Rights," with Eric Severeid and Martin Agronsky, CBS News
Special, December 3, 1968 (mimeo transcript).

trine, later termed the "preferred freedoms" doctrine, in 1938—a doctrine grown from, and now grown far beyond, Holmes' marketplace theory.

Felix Frankfurter led the challengers to Stone's position. His fullest rehearsal of the theory of judicial restraint occurred in *Minersville* v. *Gobitis* (1940)[7] and *W. Virginia* v. *Barnette* (1943),[8] both of which raised the question of whether states could require children, as conditions of public school attendance, to pledge allegiance to the U.S. flag against their religious convictions.

In *Gobitis*, the Court through Frankfurter replied in the affirmative, with Stone filing a dissent destined to become the majority view three years later. Invoking the "discrete and insular minorities" condition from footnote four, Stone reasoned that the First Amendment's protection of free exercise of religion prevented expulsion of Jehovah's Witness children for refusing homage to what they held to be a "graven image."[9] In a letter to Stone, Frankfurter outlined his agreement with the distinction in footnote four. "I regard it as basic," Frankfurter wrote. "I have taken over that distinction in its central aspect, however inadequately, in the present opinion by insisting on the importance of keeping open all those channels of free expression by which undesirable legislation may be removed, and keeping unobstructed all forms of protest against what are deemed invasions of conscience."[10]

The "discrete and insular minorities" condition in some respects looked to the same end as did political restraints. And it shared with political restraints parentage in the marketplace theory. But it did not justify special judicial power in functional terms—in terms of its contribution to the workings as opposed to the substantive results of the democratic political system. Actually, the condition seemed merely to assert in some cases a minority's right to prevail

---

[7] 310 U.S. 586. 　　　　　　　[8] 319 U.S. 624.
[9] 310 U.S. 586, 601.
[10] Full text in Alpheus T. Mason, *Security Through Freedom* (Ithaca, N.Y., 1955), pp. 217-220.

over majority will. This appeared the antithesis of democracy.

Frankfurter's theory ostensibly squared with the lessons of 1937. Democratic theory requires that political, not judicial, controls be primary. Through the franchise, the subject of power becomes the ruler or wielder of power as well. This condition is not necessarily realized when a Court, whose members are appointed with virtually life tenure, obtrudes itself between the people and the policies decided by their elected representatives. Frankfurter maintained opposition to any implication that some rights might be exempted from the lessons of 1937 regarding the limits of judicial authority. The argument culminated in Frankfurter's lecture to the Court in *Kovacs* v. *Cooper* (1948). "'Preferred freedoms,'" he wrote, ". . . is a phrase that has crept into some recent opinions of this Court. I deem it a mischievous phrase if it carries the thought, which it may subtly imply, that any law touching communication is affected with presumptive invalidity."[11]

Underlying Frankfurter's objections to preferred freedoms was the notion that "process" in and of itself imposes certain requirements on Institutional actors in the political system. Just as the electorate and the legislature must adhere to certain processes (e.g., decision-making through voting, using majority rule), so must the Court. Mechanistic use of resolving formulas led, in Frankfurter's view, to departures from judicial good form as the Court failed scrupulously to pay "alert deference" to the legislature.

But significantly, the debate hardly touched the propriety of the buyer-seller model from which all else flowed. Frankfurter attacked the libertarians' alleged departure from what he felt to be the (since 1937, at least) accepted form. Yet legislative hegemony was itself but the result of reliance on the marketplace theory as a model of the political process. Nor did any major participant in the libertarian debate question the rationalistic assumptions implicit in a view of the political process on the market model. On the contrary,

[11] 336 U.S. 77, 90.

the Court reports from the early 1940's onward are replete with affirmations of the efficacy of reasoned discourse in the political arena.[12]

The buyer-seller model, ostensibly expelled from constitutional jurisprudence through the 1937 reversals, was readmitted by way of the marketplace doctrine in the civil liberties debate. The model had become part of the body of "inarticulate major premises" of judicial decision-making. It had become a common mental set, an element of the justices' basic intellectual equipment. In response to a preferred freedoms doctrine developed by his fellow judicial *bricoleurs* from the buyer-seller mode, *Frankfurter advanced the supremacy of decision-making in the give and take of electoral bargaining—belief in whose salutary possibilities is as much a fiction fostered by the assumptions characteristic of a buyer-seller model of society as were the marketplace and preferred freedoms doctrines*. And this from judges to whom the works of LeBon and Pareto, Freud, and Madison Avenue were amply available.

For all their apparent opposition, therefore, the Stone and Frankfurter positions exemplified application, albeit differently, of similar formulas drawn in common from a view of the nature of the political transaction in the buyer-seller mode. There lay the problem. For in fact, a new political syntax was developing in the civil liberties field as in the social and economic area, around the power relationship—not around exchange—as the basic organizing principle.

[2]

New Forms of Political Communication Make the Buyer-Seller Model Simplistic and Maybe Irrelevant to Society Today

Liberty of expression no longer embraces merely the rights to talk and, if anyone wants to listen, to be heard. Peaceful

---

[12] See, e.g., *Schneiderman* v. *U. S.* 320 U.S. 118 (1943), *Dennis* v. *U. S.* 341 U.S. 494 (1951), *Barenblatt* v. *U. S.* 360 U.S. 109 (1959), Black's dissent.

picketing has long since been sustained by the Supreme Court as a legitimate exercise of free speech.[13] The Court upheld the legality of peaceful demonstrations in the early 1960's.[14] It would soon confront even farther-reaching questions of "symbolic speech" by draft-card burners purposefully violating selective service laws to protest the Vietnam War.[15] A liberalization of sexual attitudes released pressures for judicial redefinition of the relationship of First Amendment guarantees to new art forms. Such pressures led in the post-World War II decades to Court-imposed restrictions on the state censorship powers[16] that would have been unimaginable in an America closer to the Puritan wellspring of its political culture. Rioting has become a common political tactic.

Increasing political activism, especially by the young, daily raises new questions regarding the legality of mass protests, sit-ins, "participatory democracy." Such forms of political communication neither fall within the traditional buyer-seller mode, nor look to achievement of greater buyer-seller efficiency as a goal. The term "New Left" implies a demand for fundamental revisions in attitudes toward social action and organization. The New Left espousal of sexual freedom and championship of "love-motivated" behavior in reaction against materialism and institutionalized aggressiveness ("Make love, not war!") represent a mass revulsion against society as currently patterned. These may be interpreted as demands for movement toward the "commune" model and away from society as a market or domain. Demonstrations, sit-ins, student strikes and the like suggest that activists in growing numbers have given up on the efficacy of traditional political processes, the same processes on whose validity the philosophy of footnote four relies.

[13] *Thornhill* v. *Alabama*, 310 U.S. 88 (1940).

[14] *Brown* v. *Louisiana*, 383 U.S. 131 (1966).

[15] *United States* v. *O'Brien* 391 U.S. 367 (1968).

[16] See *Burstyn* v. *Wilson*, 343 U.S. 495 (1952); *Roth* v. *U. S.*, 354 U.S. 476 (1957).

In point is an exchange in early 1969 between Daniel P. Moynihan and Adam Walinsky on the use of representative channels to effect social change. Moynihan, liberal scholar and practicing bureaucrat in the Kennedy, Johnson, and Nixon administrations, in his book, *Maximum Feasible Misunderstanding*, extolled representative government as having the virtue of defining "who speaks for the community."[17] In an incisive—that is, a cutting—review of the book, Walinsky, a former aid to Senator Robert F. Kennedy, rejected the Moynihan thesis as mystical and question-begging. The Bedford-Stuyvesant black ghetto in Brooklyn, Walinsky suggested, showed the deepening irrelevance of old notions of "representative" and "community":[18]

> In the Bedford-Stuyvesant ghetto of New York there are 450,000 people—as many as in the entire city of Cincinnati, more than in the entire state of Vermont. Yet the area has only one high school, and 80 per cent of its teenagers are dropouts; the infant mortality rate is twice the national average; there are over 800 buildings, abandoned by everyone but the rats, yet the area received not one dollar of urban renewal funds during the entire first 15 years of that program's operations; the unemployment rate is known only to God.

Eschewing traditional channels, civil rights and social reform leaders turn to direct action. Citizens have created a new franchise.[19] Through this new franchise they can demonstrate beliefs and register desires more dramatically and sometimes much more effectively than through the ballot box.

The continuing relevance of traditional doctrines of the role of speech in a free society is in question. Yet such doctrines furnish the working tools of America's constitutional

[17] New York, 1969, p. 182.

[18] *New York Times Book Review*, February 2, 1969, p. 28.

[19] The "new franchise" idea was first suggested by my former colleague, Mr. Jeffrey Shane, currently in the Office of General Counsel, Department of Transportation.

bricoleurs—this in an environment marked by expanding concepts of speech, communication, and indeed of politics itself. New constitutional concepts, not the old signs, will be needed to cope with these challenges.

The framers of the Constitution were men of the Age of Reason and Enlightenment. They focused on political efficiency in a system whose basic policy goal—protection of property—was a given. Aligned by philosophy with Washington's pronouncement, "The foundation of our empire was was not laid in the gloomy age of ignorance and superstition,"[20] the framers saw free, rational political discourse among reasonable men as a means of achieving a workable system. This belief gave a decisive set to the framers' political syntax. But it is otherwise today. People are by no means convinced of their age's liberation from ignorance and superstition.

Speech, especially when considered in its "new" forms, now serves functions in addition to that of rational dialogue. Many functions of speech might indeed be considered downright irrational. They are thus far beyond the marketplace theory's ambit, which was confined to insuring communication so that political ideas would be constantly exposed to scrutiny by potential political "buyers"—the citizenry, the voters. Modern uses of speech, press, and assembly have, in other words, far outstripped the simplistic model of rational men in rational dialogue that informed the framers' design. Similarly, the concept of the "democratic processes" today must encompass more than the act of voting. We can broadly distinguish three primary uses of speech: dialogue, demonstration, and disruption.

(*a*) *Dialogue.* There is communication as dialogue, appealing to reason and seeking to influence behavior through rational persuasion. Speech in the exchange mode—an exchange of ideas—underlies the marketplace theory and gives any validity to Stone's footnote four as well as to most other libertarian theories (e.g., Cardozo's in *Palko* v. *Con-*

[20] "Circular Letter to the Governors," June 8, 1783, *Writings*, 2nd ed., 10: 254, 256.

necticut and Black's literal absolutism) that are logically consistent with Stone's contribution.

(*b*) *Demonstration.* Second, there is communication through demonstration. Demonstration aims not at persuasion through rational exchange, but at marshalling opinion by energizing the public's emotions and "better instincts." "Dialogue" is opinion education; "demonstration," opinion manipulation. This suggests a shift from the exchange to the power or control principle. Moreover, demonstration seems widely to have supplanted reliance on law—the latter is increasingly seen as ineffective or cynical, and out of touch with the urgencies—as the primary technique of the traditional American "appeal to right."

Demonstration as a form of political communication is directed less at conveying information about the demonstrators' viewpoint than at dramatizing the intensity with which they support policies or feel grievances. The function is to generate and elicit empathy. Demonstrations thus seek to provide an empirical solution to one of politics' most troublesome problems, the so-called "intensity problem," which results from the absence of any theoretically rigorous technique for measuring feeling on an interpersonal basis.[21]

(*c*) *Disruption.* Third, speech in its more activist manifestations is employed with increasing frequency to disobey laws, to disrupt the political processes. Such protests either show the disrupters' lack of faith in the processes being upset (as in sit-ins by Students for a Democratic Society at universities) or else attempt to blackmail the government with a threat ("satisfy our grievances or we will burn the country down" is widely viewed as the demand of Black militants).

The more disruptive forms of civil disobedience postulate a basic antagonism between their exponents and the representatives of inherited order. Disruption thus becomes more than a mere appeal for support, more even than revolutionary technique. It poses a continuing test of will, stam-

[21] On the "intensity problem" see Robert Dahl, *A Preface to Democratic Theory* (Chicago, 1956), esp. chap. 4.

ina, and values between the adversaries, forcing society into extended conflict with the radical dissidents until one side's nerves give out. Such attempts to move the political system by essentially coercive means makes the old free speech issues—e.g., dissemination of subversive literature, "red infiltration" of unions[22]—weak stuff indeed by comparison. Both pamphleteering and propagandizing may in fact be viewed as lying within the exchange mode. But disobedience and disruption plainly substitute ruler-subject transactions for rational persuasion. It is doubtful that these forms are even within the reach, let alone the grasp, of received constitutional doctrines tracing by way of the marketplace doctrine to the buyer-seller model.

[3]
The Basic Challenge to Constitutional Law Is to Become Itself a Force for Achievement of a New Working Political Syntax

Political democracy owes much to such economic doctrines as rationality and man's responsiveness to ordered incentive patterns, and to such values as personal freedom and the sanctity of decisions arrived at through open discussion or bargaining. American public law, similarly, has relied on the economic model for rules to govern political behavior. Yet *no more important historical paradigm is to be uncovered in American constitutional history than that of the developing awareness that ruler-subject, not buyer-seller, transactions actually dominate society.*

An appropriate jurisprudential response to this developing awareness was needed, one supplied in part by the 1937 Supreme Court decisions and those that followed. Thus the *U.S. v. Classic* (1941)[23] and *Smith v. Allwright* (1944)[24] decisions recognized that political parties discriminating against Negroes by denying participation in primaries are not mere "political marketing" agencies. They are thus

---

[22] E.g., *Gitlow v. N. Y.*, 268 U.S. 652 (1925); *American Communications Ass'n. v. Doud*, 339 U.S. 382 (1950).

[23] 313 U.S. 299.   [24] 321 U.S. 649.

exerting a kind and degree of power over persons and over the political system itself which the Constitution forbids. To the same effect, the apportionment decisions of the 1960's,[25] recognizing that shares of political power are the basic stakes in elections, enforced on state legislative elections the "one man, one vote" rule of equal power. Paradigmatic development in one area, such as voting rights, produces stresses in other areas of a political system. These stresses release sympathetic, syntactic forces which work toward restoration of thematic coherence. The so-called "New Politics" of the 1960's may be interpreted as one manifestation of such syntactic forces, whose lesson is that the old economic model is as inappropriate a matrix of rules in the civil liberties area as it was in economic and social life.

The parallel need on the legal front is to develop a constitutional jurisprudence on ruler-subject assumptions. Such assumptions must be adequate to the relations and aspirations of power characterizing the political processes in the era of a new franchise—the era of demonstration, disobedience, and disruption as well as of dialogue. A jurisprudence of concepts rather than of signs, recognizing the departures of today's politics from traditional models, looks to equally abrupt departures from inherited forms. The Court's apportionment decisions suggest movement in this direction— and with it, perhaps a judicial forsaking of the constraints of *bricolage*.

Unless law supports the development of political syntax, remaining flexible in outlook and operation as are society's rules themselves, it becomes a disintegrative force. A system of jurisprudence tends, like any other aspect of culture, to be coherent. The bias of American law, favoring rich over poor where property rights are concerned, thus carries far beyond the property field—for example, into areas of life or death in criminal law. (Almost all persons sentenced to death in American courts have been poor, uneducated, and often members of a minority. About half those waiting

[25] *Baker* v. *Carr*, 369 U.S. 186 (1962); *Reynolds* v. *Sims*, 377 U.S. 533 (1964).

execution in mid-1968 were Negroes, and more than half actually put to death have been Black.)²⁶ Accountably, therefore, impatience with traditional political and legal processes in part reflects revulsion over the fact that law in the U.S. is, to an extent altogether inconsistent with professed American values, class law. This law is dominated by categories from the buyer-seller model rather than by "fair play" notions, such as those discussed in Chapter I, which have been developed to moderate ruler-subject transactions.

Yet here too is discernible a trend toward a jurisprudence which does not hew slavishly to the old signs, forms, and fictions. As we have seen, constitutional law in the age of laissez-faire postulated a kind of *a priori* or "constructive" equality among individuals (e.g., as legal agents executing contracts). The developing jurisprudence recognizes the existence and impact of disparities in wealth, knowledge, and power. The right-to-counsel decisions, *Gideon* v. *Wainwright* (1963)²⁷ and *Miranda* v. *Arizona* (1966),²⁸ recognize that men cannot be equal before the law unless the public, by providing counsel, helps in the legal arena to redress the disadvantages of indigent or ill-educated defendants. More generally, these cases reflect the transfer to criminal justice of an insight closely associated with the New Deal's functionalist orientation.

This is the insight that society no longer consists of independent actors establishing their positions through face-to-face bargaining. It must be viewed as a network of interdependencies, often representing group interests and forces larger than the power of any individual. Society, working through these forces, shared in the formation of all the hapless limitations of its Clarence Gideons—inarticulateness, functional illiteracy, inability when accused adequately to present a fair defense.²⁹ So society should bear a fair weight

²⁶ James Duffy (Warden, San Quentin) in *New York Times*, July 7, 1968, p. 12ᴇ.

²⁷ 373 U.S. 335.   ²⁸ 384 U.S. 436.

²⁹ Anthony Lewis, *Gideon's Trumpet* (New York, 1964).

of responsibility and cost in equalizing the Gideons' chances by furnishing attorneys at trial. A similar awareness of society's interdependencies—an awareness relying on sociological data and far transcending the inherited jurisprudential "signs"—has informed judicial activity on behalf of equal opportunity among the races.[30]

Post-1930's Court departures in civil liberties, criminal justice, and race relations may be charged to two factors: first, incorporation in constitutional jurisprudence of new concepts in the strict sense (see Chapter v), expanding the categories of legal inquiry beyond the constraints of *bricolage* so they begin to reflect reality itself rather than models of reality; and second, adjustment of the law to cope with problems in a society dominated by power relationships, rather than continued reliance on a jurisprudence of economic "signs." The crucial remaining question is this: at what level of cultural integration will coercion, which is central to the concept of law, usefully support values and influence behavior?

With respect to some values, integration exists in high degree. Coercion is often unnecessary to support values so deeply held or so compellingly identified with each individual's welfare as to be almost self-enforcing. At the other extreme, coercion is often not worth its cost or trouble with respect to values on which no consensus exists. *Thus a society must constantly search for, and adjust to, the shifting intermediate level of cultural integration at which use of law as a social instrument will be both meaningful and feasible. To bring this search to a fruitful issue is the highest duty of the Supreme Court.* It is also the Court's most difficult task in a period of social volatility verging, some observers think, on outright social disintegration.

A creative jurisprudential contribution to achievement of a new syntax will test the judges' courage no less than their acumen. For the old "signs"—again in the technical

[30] Particularly in the first *Brown* v. *Board* case which decided that in the field of education, "separate" is inherently unequal. See 347 U.S. 483 (1954).

sense of Chapter v—point, surely, in the wrong direction. As yet untested concepts will be needed to effect the full transition in public law, following society's transition in fact, from buyer-seller to ruler-subject dominance. Exchange, a theoretically self-policing transaction, has given way to the power principle as the basic modifier of social interaction. This fact in itself heightens the importance of society's search, in the persons of those who interpret its laws, for new behavioral rules commanding general respect and justifying governmental enforcement.

It was pointed out in Chapter i that the Supreme Court's recent tendency to refer decisions on criminal procedure to the "rule of fair play" represents an attempt to ground constitutional jurisprudence on a single widely shared norm. Controversy as to whether or not the Court has "coddled criminals" is not over the validity of this norm, but over its application—namely, to what extent does true "fair play" as much require punishment for accused offenders as it does special solicitude for their rights? By these decisions, the Court turned from precedents supporting use of public power in ways that were perceived as discriminatory by the very groups most likely to be on the receiving end of the process. The point is not that the Supreme Court primarily meant to be discriminatory by permitting, for example, state authority to try accused persons without counsel, or to exclude objectors to the death sentence from the jury in capital cases, or to use evidence obtained by means that would be inadmissible in federal courts. But the tradition of *bricolage* tied law to conflict-resolving formulas that predated modern notions of the nature, manifestations, and impact of discrimination.

As in the criminal justice, so in other areas. To have moved from the *bricoleur's* art as the archetype of judicial form toward a jurisprudence of concepts tailored to the realities rather than the shadows of American politics, has —wisely and well—begun to move constitutional interpretation beyond the Constitution.

INDEX